RIVER *of* FORGIVENESS

K. Lorraine Kiidumae

PTP
PTP Book Division
Path to Publication Group, Inc.
Arizona

Copyright © 2021 K. Lorraine Kiidumae
Printed in the United States of America
All Rights Reserved

Cover Artist: Peter Kiidumae

This is a work of fiction. Any names or characters, businesses or places, events or incidents, are fictitious. Any resemblance to actual persons, living or dead, or actual events is purely coincidental. No part of this book may be used or reproduced by any means, graphic, electronic, or mechanical, including photocopying, recording, taping or by any information storage retrieval system without the written permission of the publisher except in the case of brief quotations embodied in articles and reviews.

Reviewers may quote passages for use in periodicals, newspapers, or broadcasts provided credit is given to *River of Forgiveness* by K. Lorraine Kiidumae and Saguaro Books, LLC.

PTP Book Division
Imprint of Saguaro Books, LLC
16845 E. Avenue of the Fountains, Ste. 325
Fountain Hills, AZ 85268
www.ptpbookdivision.com

ISBN: 9798388553744
Library of Congress Cataloging Number
LCCN: 2021940869
Printed in the United States of America
First Edition

Dedication

To My Mother, In Loving Memory.
This Book Is for You.

Acknowledgments

A big thanks to members of my Studio Nine writing group—Janie Brown, Yaana Dancer, Lara Janze, Karen J. Lee, Dhana Musil, Rua Mercier, Carrie Saxifrage, and Carol Tulpar—who have seen this book from beginning to end and provided me with their gold.

I'm grateful to the wonderful writer-mentors I worked with on this novel—Betsy Warland, Shaena Lambert and Timothy Taylor from the Simon Fraser University Writer's Studio, who read the first pages and encouraged me to continue; Claudia Casper with the Vancouver Manuscript Intensive, who advised on the first draft and pointed the way forward; Dennis Bock with the Humber School for Writers who critiqued and edited the final draft, giving me the confidence to send this story out into the world; my publisher, Mary J. Nickum with Saguaro Books, LLC for accepting and copy editing the final manuscript.

Thank you to Robert Shatzkin from Liveright Publishing Corporation, a division of W. W. Norton & Company, for granting permission to use the E. E. Cummings poems I'm honored to have included in this book.

Special thanks to my dear friends Anne Bowers, Heather Carroll, Chris Matthews, Debbie Morris, and Susan Evans-Wells (The Green Grasshopper is for you), for generously giving of their time to read and comment on the first draft of my novel, and to Helen Jantzi for her ongoing and enthusiastic support and encouragement.

To my father, Ron, my sister Sharon, my husband Peter and the many members of my extended family—thank you for always cheering me on with your endless and unwavering belief over the many years it took to complete this novel. You have my love always.

Finally, to my mother, the first love of my life and my first storyteller, thank you for the countless Sunday afternoon phone calls, lighting up my imagination with so many delightful stories, from which some of these characters were reborn.

River of Forgiveness

"Trust your heart if the seas catch fire, live by love though the stars walk backward."
– e.e. cummings

i carry your heart with me (i carry it in my heart)
i am never without it(anywhere i go you go, my dear; and
whatever is done by only me is your doing, my darling)

                                                             i fear
no fate(for you are my fate, my sweet)i want no world(for
beautiful you are my world, my true)
and it's you are whatever a moon has always meant
and whatever a sun will always sing is you

here is the deepest secret nobody knows (here is the root of the
root and the bud of the bud and the sky of the sky of a tree
called life; which grows higher than the soul can hope or mind
can hide)
and this is the wonder that's keeping the stars apart

i carry your heart(i carry it in my heart)

Kiidumae

Chapter 1
With Wings like a Ladybird

On the morning of Sydney's wedding day, a little green finch flew into the window on the back porch of the veranda, and Mum, thinking it a bad omen, became hysterical, as she is prone to be, flapping at it with the broom—"getaway, getaway, shoo, shoo," she hollered. Mum got a closer look at it and stood in a frenzy on top of the old white paint-chipped wooden chair in the veranda screaming "it's lousy, it's lousy—Ambroise, for God's sake come in here and do something."

Papa, sitting at the dining room table, his pipe puffing in his mouth, filling their little stucco house with the sweet smoky smell of tobacco, rose from his game of solitaire with a sigh, and came wearily out to the veranda. He put on his fishing gear—waterproof jacket, pants, hat with a mesh face that was to keep the mosquitoes off, boots and all. He went in with the small net he used for catching smelts and swooped the bird into it in a flash. He gently stroked the little finch's back and after a few moments rest, she recovered and flew off. Mum moaned with relief, rubbing at her neck with iodine, to soothe her rising blood pressure, a curse since she'd contracted Scarlett Fever, as a girl, back home in Scotland. Papa walked back to the dining room table, to his unfinished game.

Later that same day, Sydney's wedding day, everyone who'd attended said it had been the blood-curdling sound of Mum's bawling, reverberating off the stained-glass ceiling of St. Patrick's Cathedral as they were ushered silently out the doors, that stayed with them. Haunted them.

It haunted everyone afterward because it was that same bawling Mum had done thirteen years earlier, at the Wesley Street United Church on the day Ambroise James Archambault Jr. was christened. He was a month old and, later, seemed to mean more to Mum than all three of her girls combined. And it was the saddest of days for, not only was it the day of his christening, but it was also the day of his funeral. The baby boy, so cherished, so rejoiced over in the Archambault household—his birth marked by Papa bringing out his Chateau Julien cigars—the finest longleaf, Cuban-seed tobacco, stored in his humidor along with his pipe tobacco, handed out to everyone

Kiidumae

who arrived at the house to congratulate them on the birth of their son; the cigars served with some of the Cointreau from the dining room cabinet, poured out sparingly into Mum's cordial glasses—until one morning little Ambroise Jr. did not wake up when Mum went to get him from his crib.

"The pastor at the hospital thinks it best—that it would aid in Mum's grieving and healing—to have a funeral," Papa said. And so, on that same day as he was to be christened, Mum dressed Ambroise James Archambault Jr. in the long, white satin gown she'd ordered, made especially for him for christening. His soft dark curls peeked out beneath his bonnet, a feature at birth, a full head of hair, such a beautiful baby he'd been, everyone said so.

"He looks like a girl, wearing that silly dress," Sydney hissed, as he was carried down the aisle to the front of the church.

Afterward, Mum was never really herself again—"it was the post-partum on top of everything else," Aunt Bessie said later when she'd come all the way down on the train from Winnipeg to help out. Mum took straight to her bed, as soon as Aunt Bessie arrived, and lay there, day after day, night after night, in the dark, clutching onto a locket of baby Ambroise's hair and the blanket she'd brought him home from the hospital in after he was born. It frightened Sydney. She was only just five years old then. A grey hush settled in over their little stucco house on Cumberland Street, and Sydney wished Ambroise James Archambault Jr. had never been born.

River of Forgiveness

Maisie was practically still a baby herself then, just nineteen months old, and after a few weeks, Mum clung to the poor child as if she was all she had left. Alone in her bedroom with Maisie, Mum fed and changed and cooed over her, focusing on her, tending to her needs—the two of them lost to the world.

Sydney loitered outside the bedroom door, continuously trying the handle of the doorknob, but it was kept locked. Mum seemed to have forgotten she was even there. She slunk to the floor and held her ear to the door, listening, waiting. Sydney sat, rubbing the tears from her eyes with her fists until Aunt Bessie softly tip-toed over and took her by the hand, shushing her with a finger against her lips.

"Dorothy's just about gone right out of her mind, poor thing," Aunt Bessie bemoaned, of Mum. She shook her head, back and forth, slowly, one hand on her hip over a yellow floral apron. She was leaning on the fence, standing among a bed of snap peas in the garden in the back yard, speaking in low tones to Spencer Frye's mother next door.

Later, when she'd come back into the kitchen, Aunt Bessie whispered warily into the telephone on the dining room wall, "I think it's some sort of a transference that has taken place." She said this to Uncle Thierry, who was Papa's brother and Aunt Bessie's husband of thirteen years. He was calling from Winnipeg. "But there's no harm in it, I suppose, and, God willing, she's bound to get better in time."

Every morning, Aunt Bessie gently shook Sydney awake and took care of her for the day while Mum was busy with Maisie. After a breakfast of cream of wheat cereal and prunes spooned out of a tin, force-fed into Sydney's scowling mouth—"they're good for you," Aunt Bessie would chuckle—she bathed her in the tub. Sydney giggled as she was rubbed down, from head to foot, dried off with a thick, terry towel that tickled her skin. Aunt Bessie helped her select a dress to wear from her closet, pulling it over Sydney's head, strapping up her shoes then giving her a kiss on the cheek as Sydney opened the screen door when Aunt Bessie sent her out into the backyard to play with Spencer Frye.

It was on one of those mornings, after Sunday school when Sydney had gone outside to play with Spencer Frye, that everything suddenly took an unexpected turn. A large puddle had formed from the spring rain, at the end of the lane in the back yard, next to the alley behind their house. Sydney and Spencer removed their clothes, folding them neatly and laying them out with their shoes on the stones, and jumped into the puddle to play. Mum happened to be up, out of her bedroom on one of those rare occasions, in the kitchen, warming a bottle for Maisie. She spotted them through the kitchen window. Sydney looked up to see Mum, racing down the stone path in the back garden, her large frame swaddled in an apron, struggling to overtake Sydney's small, child's body, with short legs flying, out of the puddle and into the alley, her Beverley doll still grasped in her right hand, held high overhead to prevent it from falling. The wooden spoon flailing, menacingly, threateningly, Sydney's eyes large with fear as she turned to see if she had reached the end of her beating. They'd removed their freshly pressed clothes, to preserve them, and thought they'd be praised but Mum went right out of her head and began swatting Sydney over and over again, all over her naked body, with the wooden spoon, until her flesh was red and sore. Spencer grabbed his suit and shoes and ran to his house and slammed the door shut.

Papa, sitting at the dining room table, the pipe puffing, the cards laid out—too important, too all-encompassing—to leave and come to her rescue.

"Isn't she a little...a little...overly spirited?" Papa said to Aunt Bess afterward.

"Ah, tsk, she's just expressing herself," Aunt Bessie said.

Papa seemed lost in a stupor without Mum there to manage things, the way she usually did. In the evenings, when he returned to the house after work, before he'd even had any supper, he wandered off down the street to visit with Mr. Napier a few blocks over (whose wife had recently given birth to a baby as well) to commiserate over Ambroise Jr.'s loss. Otherwise, it was all he could do to cope with his job as a carpenter at the shipyard.

Left behind to run the Mulberry Bush—Uncle Thierry and Aunt Bessie's small consignment children's clothing store at Portage and Main—after a few weeks Uncle Thierry could no longer cope with the demands himself and, thus, after the incident in the puddle, it was decided there was nothing else to do but pack Sydney's little brown and tan tweed suitcase and take her with them.

"It's just for a time," Aunt Bessie said. "Just until your Mum's back on her feet again."

At first, Sydney was excited about the train ride to Winnipeg, about the packing of her five-year-old's belongings into the little suitcase, emptying her piggy bank of all its jangling coins to take with her, wrapping her Beverley doll in a blanket, and carrying her under her arm for the journey. But almost as soon as she arrived at Uncle Thierry and Aunt Bessie's quiet, small brick bungalow, Sydney wanted to go back home again.

Uncle Thierry and Aunt Bessie had no children of their own; everything in their living room was just so, with crocheted white and ecru doilies, each hand made by Aunt Bess to the right size for what sat upon them. Everything was still; Sydney heard the sound of the clock ticking back and forth above the mantle on the fireplace.

When Uncle Thierry wasn't working at the Mulberry Bush, he sat in his worn rocker and read his books. There was a wall of thick books behind his chair and he mulled through them with an air of contentment until he settled on the right one. An old phonograph someone had left on the back step of the Mulberry Bush early one morning, played a seventy-eight from a stack in a cardboard box in the corner, abandoned along with the phonograph. All of the records were classical music and Uncle Thierry seemed to particularly like Chopin, the Nocturnes. To Sydney, their living room seemed like someplace foreign. She missed Mum and she missed Maisie and she missed Papa. She didn't understand why she'd been sent away. A feeling of panic began to set in.

River of Forgiveness

"Events that happen pass away and are gone before you know it," Aunt Bessie said, in an effort to console her. "At the time, they seem as though they will last forever. Later, they are nothing but a distant, fond, memory. This, you can count on."

Papa wrote—"to My Dearest Little Sydney"—and then, quoting from her favorite nursery rhyme, "'with wings like a ladybird', you'll return home soon. Be brave and show Aunt Bess what a strong, well-behaved girl you can be."

The weeks went on and Aunt Bessie, not knowing what else to do, took Sydney to the Mulberry Bush and set her to work, removing buttons from blouses and jackets that had a few missing ones, replacing them with new sets taken from other worn garments, or containers of buttons from the Salvation Army.

Papa's letters dwindled in frequency over time and then one day Sydney heard Uncle Thierry and Aunt Bessie tsk, tsking over one they'd received in the mail. He was at his wits' end, Papa said, and Aunt Bessie lowered her voice then, into an alarmingly hushed tone. She gasped, as she told Uncle Thierry there was word from Ambroise that Mum was still breastfeeding Maisie, now almost three and a half years old. The neighbors feared Mum might be going a little mad.

"Why she's gone right out of her toque," Aunt Bessie exclaimed to Uncle Thierry.

She forced a smile when she looked down and saw Sydney behind her, looking up with an ashen face. Then Aunt Bessie began humming nervously, pretending she was checking on the bread baking in the oven.

Soon afterward, another letter arrived. Aunt Bessie bobbed up and down excitedly as she read it, flapping the parchment it was written on, at a loss for words. 'Dorothy is saved by the news of another baby to come,' Papa had told them gleefully in the letter.

The baby Mum was expecting was to be Deirdre, who they later nick-named Deedee because she hated her given name but, at the time Mum had her hopes set on another boy. Uncle Thierry began to complain he feared they may never send for Sydney. She seemed to have been forgotten but Aunt Bessie told her later that secretly she'd hoped they'd be able to keep her.

"I'm beginning to like having a good-natured little girl around the house," she said.

Sydney almost began to feel as though she belonged to Aunt Bess now but Mum and Papa weren't providing any money or any other form of compensation for her care—"they likely think we can afford to keep on feeding her since we don't have any of our own," Sydney overheard Uncle Thierry say.

All the news on the radio began to upset Uncle Thierry after that, and he spoke of it constantly—there was talk of fear of another depression and the falling of the stock market, talk of the banks failing and unemployment running above twenty percent, of war clouds gathering in Europe—and it made him increasingly anxious.

"It's just not fair. It's not right to pass on the responsibility for your child to someone else," Uncle

River of Forgiveness

Thierry griped. His grumbling increased by the day after he'd had news of the impending baby to come and so, in a matter of months, 'with wings like a ladybird', Sydney was sent home again, just after Deedee was born.

She was glad to be back in their little stucco house on Cumberland Street, their house that had remained so grand, so large in her memory, but was actually, she discovered upon her return, really quite small. She was glad to be back to Papa's pipe, always in his mouth, and the sweet smoky smell of his tobacco but she felt as a visitor might in her old bedroom that Maisie had gotten used to having to herself. There was plenty to do around the house though, with Maisie now a preschooler and Deedee just an infant. Mum soon engaged Sydney in warming bottles and changing and washing diapers. She hummed Uncle Thierry's tunes to herself as she worked, to stave off the monotony.

She missed being with Uncle Thierry and Aunt Bessie and their quiet, gentle ways, much more than she had anticipated and, for a while, she was sad not to be with them. For, as stiff as they were, they'd been kind to her and she longed for the peace of being an only child with all the attention.

Those summer days Sydney had spent outside in their garden, in the sunshine, watching, listening, running across to the other side of the yard when she saw a small, red, speckled ladybug alight on a leaf, or scratch in the dirt in the cracks of the sidewalk, trying to see its wings. The endless music of Uncle Thierry's records wafting out through the open window— Chopin and the Nocturnes.

Kiidumae

Deedee proved to be a bit of a poor sickly little thing, regularly catching pneumonia in the wintertime. Mum was busy cooking and taking care of Maisie, who was "attached at the hip," to Mum now, as Papa always said. "It's unnatural how that girl clings to her mother."

Of course, it was Sydney who was expected to hold vigil at Deedee's bedside each winter, keeping a cold compress on her forehead, reading her stories to keep her mind attuned, watching the unsteadiness of her breathing. She was always at the ready with a hot bowl of tomato soup or a tomato sandwich when she finally opened her eyes. When Deedee started kindergarten, Sydney rose early each morning to walk her to school.

For almost as long as she could remember, Sydney had always felt she'd had to look after herself. She knew that, with Mum and Papa, she always would be. She yearned for someone to cherish her and dote on her as Mum did on Maisie, as she did for Deedee. The way, for that brief time, Aunt Bessie and Uncle Thierry had on her.

"'With wings like a ladybird' Sydney, you'll come home to me," Papa had said and now, here she was.

Chapter 2
At the Dance

It was one day when Sydney came home from school for lunch that they first met. She walked into the kitchen and found him there, sitting at the table, eating a bowl of soup and a chunk of Mum's homemade bread.

"Ah, there you are," Mum cooed when Sydney walked in. Her friend Helka had forgotten her hat that day and they'd gone back to the school to get it, so Sydney was late.

"Look who's here," Mum flushed when she'd introduced him. "Look who we have in the house now—it's a Limey, all the way over from England. We can hardly understand each other though," Mum giggled akin to a schoolgirl and looked the happiest Sydney had ever seen her, for as long as she could remember, anyway.

"Ah, get out, you Scotty's can't even pronounce your o's—everything's the beau—like "the beaut" instead of "the boat," the man seated at the table said.

"Aw, you," Mum said. "You're one to talk. There wouldn't even be an England, were it not for Queen Elizabeth the First having the gumption to kill off Mary, Queen of Scots. Oh, but where's my manners?" Mum said, suddenly remembering Sydney. "This is Mister Elliott Caldwell," she said.

All of Uncle Thierry's fears he'd listened to on the radio had come to pass and, since the recession, Mum had taken to inviting a regular stream of hobos in for soup when they came to the door. With no work and no prospects at home, these vagrants travelled for free by freight train, landing in Current River to try their luck. Now Sydney wondered whether this stranger sitting here wasn't another one of them.

"As Jesus said, the second great commandment is 'Thou shalt love thy neighbor as thyself,'" Mum had often said of these men if ever Sydney admonished her for her foolishness in trusting them.

"It's not as if we don't have enough chores to do around here already, without having to feed the entire neighborhood too," Sydney grumbled to Maisie and Deedee when she, as the eldest, was conscripted to the kitchen each evening after supper to help Mum make a large pot of soup.

River of Forgiveness

Things had been different once Sydney returned home from Winnipeg. Mum's trauma since losing Ambroise Jr. seemed to manifest itself somewhere between love and empathy for mankind and an obsessive strictness and over-protectiveness toward her own children.

Sydney wasn't sure if it was because of Ambroise Jr. or the economic recession, or both, but there were no more birthday parties anymore either, or gifts at Christmas. That first Christmas, after she'd come home, there was no longer even the pretense of Santa Claus and there was no Christmas tree in the living room with presents stacked underneath, as there used to be or there was at Uncle Thierry and Aunt Bess's house.

That first Christmas home, they'd each been given a woolen stocking with a Mandarin orange in the toe, a handful of mixed nuts still in their shell, a few peppermint candies and a white Gideon's bible with the New Testament. The bibles, their only gifts, weren't wrapped in anything other than the matching sock to their stocking.

They'd been made to gather in the living room, the three girls lined up on the sofa after breakfast and each read a passage from the Bible. Afterward, Mum said the Lord's Prayer as they kneeled on the floor with heads bowed and hands clasped. Sydney had felt nostalgic and prayed under her breath to be returned to Uncle Thierry's ritual of listening to Handel's Messiah on Christmas morning while drinking a rum and eggnog and opening their gifts.

Kiidumae

Just when Sydney thought things couldn't possibly get any worse, Mum made them get on their hands and knees after they finished reading their bibles, clean and scrub all the floors in the house, then they'd had to take down and wash all the curtains. "To give thanks to the Dear Lord, before the evening meal," Mum said.

Sydney had been afraid that Mum wouldn't let her play with Spencer Frye anymore either, when she got back, because of what happened in the puddle, "No, no, no. No daughter of mine is going to turn out to be a heathen," was all she remembered Mum shouting that day, as she'd walloped her with the wooden spoon. In Mum's eyes, boys were sacred though, and she seemed to hold no malice toward Spencer Frye.

"He's a Godsend; like being given back the son we lost," Mum and Papa both said, teary-eyed.

Spencer had taken it upon himself to help with the chores after Sydney left—cutting the grass, carrying the garbage from the house to the back lane, or working side by side along with Papa to fix a broken chair.

Spencer had grown by the time Sydney had come home anyway, into that awkward stage, where they were both too old to play together anymore. He was bigger, broader and his straight sandy hair, parted to the side, hung in his blue-gray eyes that seemed to look shyly at her now.

He sat at the desk behind her at school now too. He teased her and pulled her hair or toyed with the zipper on the back of her dress. Sydney often turned back and scowled at him but, still, she felt an unmistakable sadness, an irrational feeling that everyone she'd ever loved was going to leave her, including him, when, at the age of sixteen, on the day their school pictures were handed out, he asked if they could exchange one with each other.

"What do you want a picture of me for? We can look at each other's ducky faces every day of the week if we want to," Sydney said.

"Yeah, well, not for long," Spencer said. "I've enlisted. I'm going overseas, as soon as school's out."

"Why did you go and do that? Do you want to get yourself killed?" Sydney almost started to cry and she felt angry with him yet she wasn't sure why.

"No, I won't. I'll be back, don't worry. I don't know, Frenchie, I want to see the world. I feel like I need to do something in the war. I want to serve my country, as my father did. Besides, what else is there to do around here, anyway?" Spencer said.

He'd taken to calling her Frenchie—or worse, Frog—over the last few years. He was the only one who did and generally it annoyed her; but that day, she found she'd started liking it, his affection, as though a part of her belonged to him.

So, when Sydney saw Mum standing there next to Elliott Caldwell, looking happier than she'd ever seen her, she'd felt both a rush of gratitude and curiosity at seeing Mum so joyful and a sense of betrayal to Spencer. He was the one she said was a Godsend. He was the one she'd welcomed as her lost son but Sydney had never seen Mum fawn over him as she did with this English stranger.

Kiidumae

Elliott Caldwell looks to be quite a bit older than I am Sydney thought—*maybe even close to thirty*. He was a tall man with dark brown eyes, almost black, and dark curly hair, similar to hers, neatly trimmed and coiffed. He had an easy smile and a fresh scent of manly soap about him. He rose when he greeted her and looked her straight in the eye. "So lovely to meet you," he said, in his English accent. His charm made her flush and turn her head away and a rush of excitement rippled through her.

"He's no cockney, that one," Mum said after he left. "No, that one's a gentleman. Educated too, I'm guessing."

"So, what's an educated Englishman doing in Current River begging for soup then?" Sydney said.

"Uh, no. No. He came to the door selling those new little round glass things, those door viewers—Papa calls them peepholes—the ones you put on your front door so you can look through and see who's there," Mum said. "Mr. Caldwell said there's been forced break-ins with some of the hobos, up from Current River, 'desperate men do desperate things,' he said; but I said I didn't need one of those gadgets, that God was protecting us, looking out for our little family. He insisted though, so I told him I couldn't afford one and when I offered him a bowl of soup and some lunch instead, he said he'd put one in for me anyway, in exchange for me advertising it to the neighbors, telling them about it." Mum chuckled at her own sense of cleverness and at the needlessness of such things.

River of Forgiveness

It was a few months later, that Sydney saw Elliott Caldwell again. She and Helka were at the Wesley Street United Church, where they went for the weekly Saturday night dances. She'd first met Helka the week after she got back from Winnipeg—'the only daughter of Finns', as Mum called them—Finnish immigrants—and she and Sydney had been inseparable ever since. Sydney was working the coat check that night and had arrived early and was playing the piano until the band started. Elliott appeared in the middle of her choppy rendition of the Moonlight Sonata that Aunt Bess had taught her. He walked over, without removing his coat, and joined her at the piano. He played classical music too, similar to the kind Uncle Thierry used to listen to on his records. Everyone gathered around listening anyway, mesmerized by this beautiful English gentleman who was smiling, enraptured, as though he'd waited his entire life to find a piano again.

Afterward, when the band started, Elliott spotted Sydney at the coat check and beamed broadly at her. He seemed happy to see her and looked relieved, almost as though he'd been searching for her. Sydney had just turned seventeen on her last birthday and she couldn't see why he would be interested in her.

Sydney wasn't one of the girls who stood in front of the band and waited to be asked to dance. It wasn't that she was shy, reserved perhaps, but she was not the sort to parade in front of men. Instead, when she wasn't working at the coat check, Sydney sat at the back of one of the tables around the room, smiling, sipping on iced tea, content to watch the people and the band until she was properly introduced. It was on account of that very reserve; Elliott Caldwell told her later, he'd singled her out. Some sort of an instant attraction to her goodness.

Helka filled in for her, at the coat check, and Sydney and Elliott danced that first night, their bodies first at more of a distance, then later, closer, the tip of his nose resting on her neck in such a way as to give rise to feelings Sydney had never before encountered.

The room was plain, with no windows and an old worn wooden dance floor, dimly lit. The band played a slow song softly in the background and it all seemed magical to Sydney, as though that room had suddenly been transformed.

"You have bedroom eyes," Elliot told her, "beautiful brown bedroom eyes," he said as he looked down into them, holding her face in his hands.

She'd wondered then, just for a second—something had flickered in his eyes—whether he was what Mum thought—whether he was the educated English gentleman Mum seemed to think he was; but in the dim light and his brown-black eyes, Sydney saw the first stirrings of love. He kissed her goodbye gently, first with a slight touch on each of her cheeks, then lightly on her lips. Afterward, she was unable to stop thinking of him.

Chapter 3
The Catholics and the Protestants

Years later, after Sydney was with Elliott Caldwell that first night, at the church dance and, at the end of that evening, when he'd kissed her on the cheeks, gently, tenderly, during their first dance, she realized that she knew she'd found what she'd been waiting for her whole life. She had never felt more loved by anyone than she did at that moment. *Maybe this is what love is, and always will be, all my life*, she'd thought.

Over the next few months, Elliott was away a lot, travelling from town to town on business, selling his door viewers. Sydney waited for him eagerly, looking forward to his return. When they were together, they walked hand in hand along the river on Sunday afternoons, kissing under the lilac trees, sometimes going to the movies, and always to the Saturday night dances at the church.

Sydney was in her last year of high school and had many would-be suitors, boys who asked her out. One bought her a string of pearls. She'd smiled coyly at him and accepted his gift but her heart was only true to Elliott Caldwell. She'd never been with any other boy. Her love for Elliott made her confidence swell and her skin glow. Her smile attracted many to her.

She'd exchanged a few letters with Spencer while he was away in the army but Spencer was only a friend. She loved him, yes, but for her, there were no sparks. Their letters were not romantic. **So, what's it like over there**, she'd ask him. Or **What's it like being in the army?** Spencer never answered her questions directly; he'd joke and tease, the way he usually did, and Sydney could picture his smile, his tanned skin, the crinkle around his eyes. **Well, one thing's for sure, I never again in my life want to eat mutton,** he wrote. He'd sign his letters, **Love Always, Spencer** but, still, Sydney knew they were only good friends.

Once, after he'd been gone about a year, right before she'd met Elliott, Spencer asked in one of his letters if she'd met anyone yet. When she told him she hadn't, he wrote to say he was going to have to marry her then because he'd been the first boy ever to see her naked and that had made her laugh.

River of Forgiveness

When she graduated from high school a few months after her eighteenth birthday, Sydney and Helka found work in the hospital laundry, scrubbing and bleaching bed sheets and towels. Maisie was out of high school then too, having dropped out before she'd graduated, and she joined them at the laundry. They were each given white uniforms, similar to the ones the nurses wore, and white shoes. Sydney liked the feeling of purpose the uniform gave her—purpose and worth. She was earning money for the first time too and appreciated the sense of power it gave her, the independence. She spent very little of it—she'd bought herself a few new sweaters and dresses to wear when she was with Elliott. The rest of her earnings, she saved; she tucked the money into the back of her lingerie drawer, counting it each week and keeping a tally of her growing purse.

"Never trust the banks," Papa had told her after the recession started. Most people had kept the faith and left their money in the bank and lost everything; but Papa had kept most of his cash in Mum's old chipped blue-and-white sugar jar, hidden in the kitchen cupboard behind the honey and other condiments. So, between that and his work at the shipyard, where he was kept employed by the Government throughout the war, their family had fared better than most.

Sydney didn't say but, secretly, after the first night she'd gone to Elliott Caldwell's apartment, she was saving for herself and Elliott to buy a small house together, akin to Mum and Papa's.

The first time she went with Elliott to his apartment, Sydney looked up at the cross hanging over his bed and her mother's words whispered away, as she flushed hot with guilt.

"Why buy the cow when you can get the milk for free?" Mum's words of warning spoke to her in the back of her head. They'd left the dance at the Legion Hall early, giving them a few hours before Sydney's curfew time of midnight, when she was to be delivered back safely onto her front porch. She heard the words in her mind as she stood in Elliott's room, looking around while waiting for him to come out of the bathroom.

As soon as she looked at Elliott though, when he emerged from the bathroom, when he reached for her and she felt his fingers strum along the nape of her neck, Mum's words were forgotten. She thought about Elliott constantly when they were apart but Sydney was still always amazed at the effect he had on her when she saw him.

He removed his shoes. She had never seen him in his socks before. Something about the closeness made her feel weak and vulnerable. He took off his suit jacket and removed his tie. His crisp white shirt was tucked into his black slacks. He was a little flushed from the shot of cherry brandy they'd just shared. His complexion was a light brown against the white of his shirt. His dark eyes, almost black in the low light, were filled with a look of tenderness.

Sydney felt a pull, as gravity, in the center of her groin, and then the rush of excitement went through her and landed as butterflies in her stomach. She almost reached out for him but restrained herself at the last moment. Elliott placed his hands possessively on her shoulders and pulled her toward him. He kissed her deeply and she felt his firm tongue on hers, then the sweet taste of cherry brandy mixed with her own.

Elliott unbuttoned his shirt and Sydney touched the skin on his muscular back underneath. Her hands trembled. He pulled off her brown cardigan sweater, still kissing her, and unbuttoned the back of her dress. His hands trembled too. He laid her down on the bed. Sydney watched as Elliott placed a record onto the turntable. Chopin's *Nocturne* filled the room and she smiled at the recognition. Elliott lay down on the bed next to her and she felt his body against hers.

Sydney picked up Elliott's hand, laying it across her stomach, and held it in hers. She ran her fingers softly along the contours of his thumb and fingers. She stroked the soft little dark hairs on top of his skin.

"You have beautiful hands. Even if you hadn't already told me, I would have known you played the piano, by the perfect shape of them," Sydney said softly. She looked up into his eyes. "Yours are expressive and graceful."

A flurry of kisses ensued, the buttons on her blouse and skirt undone, Elliott's pants slid down onto the floor, and Sydney's mother's words of warning remained forgotten. Elliott kissed her cheeks softly and behind her ears then the nape of her neck, giving her goosebumps all over. He slid over top of her and Sydney felt the hairs and thick warm skin on Elliott's legs and chest against her body then his naked manliness was there. It both pleased and startled her. With agonizing reluctance, she pushed him away, remembering.

Elliott lay back for a few moments with one arm holding his head on the pillow, and smiled broadly, with a cocky look of expectant self-satisfaction across his face. Sydney laid her hand on top of his, nuzzling her cheek against his hairy chest, strumming her fingers across the top of his hand, smiling too. He entwined his fingers in hers and squeezed. He rolled on his side and kissed her, opening her mouth up to him at his lips' touch. He moaned.

"Oh Sydney. I want you so badly. I need you." She saw the shine in his dark eyes looking down hopefully at her in the dark, his face right next to hers. "Will you marry me?" he whispered.

A surge of emotion flushed through her. She felt tears of happiness in her eyes. She didn't want to disappoint him. She grabbed onto Elliott's back and held him tightly against her. He kissed her again. Sydney had never felt such love, such a desire to connect. This closeness, this need, filled her also with an inexplicable sense of despair and foreboding. She feared this feeling might slip right away again.

"Epiderm to epiderm," Elliott Caldwell said, as he made love to her, kissing and nuzzling his nose into her clean hair, inhaling the fresh scent of her shampoo. "You and me, Sydney. Flesh against flesh."

He kissed her eyelids slowly then her cheeks and lips, moving down along the tip of her ears to her neck. She felt a tingling sensation as blood rushed through her body. She leaned over and clicked off the lamp on the night table, shy of him seeing her under the sheet. She shivered as he kissed her breasts and nipples, tensing with excitement when his lips lingered on her navel, forming a circle around her belly button. She held her breath and her heart pounded into her chest.

"You are my beautiful Gypsy Savage," he laughed, rubbing his hands appreciatively over her flattened stomach, tickling her ribs. "And I will be your prince," he boasted, "and mount you on my stallion, my glossy black stallion, and ride away with you, on the saddle behind me, down to the stones along the river, where we will travel together and discover life and all there is to know, without the need ever to return to this, without the need to live an existence of such mediocrity. Ha," he cried, throwing his arm into the air, mocking the thrust of a rein. Sydney giggled and held on, to keep his hands from tickling her again, stroking her fingers through his hair in anticipation. He kissed her thighs, slowly, lingering down to her calves then jumped out of bed. He held one of her feet between his warm hands and kissed the tips of her toes. "Such small, delicate feet. Roman feet," he said, kissing them again. He crawled back into bed next to her, wrapping his naked body around her as a protective shell. She beamed silently. He had asked her to marry him. So, everything was all right. She felt vindicated and sure about her own judgment.

Sydney dozed off with Elliott holding her in his arms until she felt him gently shake her awake. Reluctantly they rose and dressed again then Elliott walked Sydney home in the dark along the bridge past Current River, under the stars, their bodies bumping softly against one another. They sauntered, holding hands then arm in arm, with Sydney smiling up at Elliott, hardly able to believe the wonderful dream her life had suddenly become.

When Sydney and Elliott got to the gate in front of her house, they sat on the front porch for a while, savoring the warm night. This feeling was all-new for Sydney. This was what it was like. She smiled. For the first time, she felt to be a woman.

Deedee walked up the path to the front porch, escorted by Mr. Napier, their neighbor three blocks over, where Deedee had been babysitting for the evening. Mr. Napier waved to Sydney and said good night then turned and headed back down the street toward home.

Sydney introduced Elliott to Deedee, beaming with an uncharacteristic glow.

"Well, well, well," he said, smirking. "So, this is Sydney's little sister." Deedee squirmed and blushed. She had turned thirteen on her birthday last September and Sydney noticed she'd been shy around strange men the last little while. "And who was that?" he asked, motioning with his hand off in the direction from which Deedee had just come. "That fellow you were with looked pretty old to be dating such a young girl." Elliott winked at Sydney.

Deedee glared at Elliott with disgust. "He was walking me home," Deedee mumbled, reluctantly, incensed she had to explain herself to this stranger. "After babysitting," she added, with emphasis.

"Ah," Elliott said, looking Deedee straight in the eye. "You'd better watch out then. He might have more on his mind than just walking you home." Elliott turned and winked at Sydney again, with a grin on his face. Sydney chuckled, hesitantly, and rose to her feet, shifting, sensing Deedee's discomfort.

"Oh, that is a disgusting thing to say," Deedee snapped back at him, her cheeks flushing red with embarrassment, searching out Sydney's eyes for moral support then, looking as though she might cry, she ran inside the house and slammed the door.

Elliott stood to go, shaking out his cramped knees then leaned forward with a self-satisfied expression, grinning boyishly, and pulled Sydney toward him to kiss her good night. Reluctantly, in a dreamy mood, she went inside and closed the door.

After he was gone, she thought over what had happened on the porch and felt confused. For an instant, she'd seen something ugly in him, a part glimpsed for the first time. Quickly she chose to forget it though, dismissing it, choosing instead to bask in the glow of their night spent together at his apartment.

She didn't feel the least bit sleepy. She went into the bedroom she shared with Deedee and quietly closed the door, not wanting to wake Mum and Papa. Deedee, still pouting over the incident on the porch, was putting on her pajamas.

"Who. Was. That?" she hissed.

"That," said Sydney, falling back onto her side of the bed, still wearing her dress, smiled dreamily. "Is—get this—my fiancé."

"What?" Deedee screeched. "What do you mean? What are you talking about?"

"Shhh. You'll wake Mum and Papa," Sydney scolded. "Tonight." She lowered her voice to a whisper, becoming serious and sentimental. "He asked me tonight."

"But you hardly know him. You've only just met him. Shouldn't you court for four or five years, like they do in a Jane Austen novel?"

"You'll see, Deedee, when it's your turn, you will see. When you meet the right man and you fall in love—no, when you rise to love—you will see. You just know, Deedee. You just know when you have found the right one."

"Well, congratulations then, I guess. I'm happy for you. If you think…if you feel…if you know he's the right one for you…I will be happy for you."

"Oh Deedee," Sydney beamed, throwing her arms around her sister. "Yes. Yes, he is." They hugged and, at last overcome with all the emotions of the day, Sydney cried happily, wiping her eyes on her dress.

"Ugh," said Deedee.
"What?"
"What is that smell?"

Sydney laughed, then blushed. She beamed. "Oh, you'll find out about that soon enough too Deedee— when it's your time."

"It smells like the kitchen after Papa cleans smelts for breakfast," Deedee said, with a quizzical expression on her face. "When will you tell Mum and Papa all this then?"

"In the morning, first thing, over breakfast. I will tell them—I'll tell them I'm engaged to be married."

Sydney lay awake all night, thinking of her life to be, her life to come; to all the things she suddenly had to look forward. Marriage. A home of her own. A man she loved. Children. All she had ever hoped for; in one day, her life had gone from ordinary, to extraordinary.

Chapter 4
Deedee Keeps a Secret

It took forever for the week to go by, until Saturday night and the next Legion dance when Sydney could see Elliott again. He had called very early the next morning, after the proposal, and woken up everyone in the house. Sydney heard the *thump, thump* of Mum's bulk, as she groped for her housecoat behind the bedroom door. Fearing it might be Elliott, Sydney leapt out of bed and ran for the phone. She wanted to be the first to tell Mum and Papa the news herself.

"Who is that, calling at this ungodly hour?" Mom commanded as she rumbled down the hallway.

"Oh, it's only Helka," Sydney lied. "She had a bad date last night."

Kiidumae

"For heaven's sake," Mum grumbled. "Foolish young girl. I'm glad none of mine are boy crazy like that." She stomped into the kitchen and lit the stove for the kettle.

Sydney had to whisper into the receiver of the telephone in the dining room, right next to the kitchen. Elliott was calling to tell her to hold off informing her parents about the wedding until he'd bought a proper engagement ring. He wanted it to be official. He wanted to be a gentleman, he said, and to ask her father for her hand but first, he needed to save for a few months to get her a ring.

Sydney felt her bubble of excitement dissipate. "I don't care about an old ring. It's you that I want. The ring doesn't matter. You can get one later, before the wedding."

Elliott went quiet for several seconds on the other end of the phone. "It matters to me," he said, finally. He hesitated. "I want you to be my wife, Sydney and I want it all to be right."

"Well," she said, pouting, not relenting. She had been awake all night long, bubbling over with excitement, waiting to tell Mum and Papa at breakfast. "I've already told Deedee, so we have to tell everyone else. Deedee can't keep a secret about anything for more than five minutes."

Elliott yelped into the phone. "Why did you have to go and tell her already?"

Sydney was alarmed at Elliott's anger. She went silent and swallowed hard to keep herself from crying.

"You're just going to have to tell Deedee to keep quiet about this for now." He softened his tone—"Until I can save enough money to buy you a ring. That just has to be the way it is."

Sydney melted a little at the thought of Elliott proposing to her properly, perhaps surprising her with a little ring box over dinner at the Black Fox Inn. She pictured herself dancing around the kitchen table, showing off her diamond to her sisters.

"All right then," she said. "I'll think of something to keep Deedee quiet. Something she's done that she won't want me to tell."

Elliott's tone lifted. "Oh, good then. That's my girl. That's my Sydney. I'll meet you on Saturday then—I'll pick you up at the door." Elliott was quiet for a few moments.

Sydney's stomach tightened, and she felt a little queasy. "Are you angry with me? Are you upset about something? Oh, I'm so sorry if I've made you cross. I simply couldn't bear it if you were unhappy." Sydney pictured him there, with his dark eyes brooding.

"No, no. I just wanted…I wondered…"

"What? What is it?"

"Well, Loves, what if, rather than us going to the dance at the Legion on Saturday night, what if we come to my apartment again, instead? I could swing by and pick you up?"

It was Sydney's turn to be silent—she was taken aback, at him being so brazen. At her perceived insinuation of his expectation of her to be unchaste again before they were married.

She looked around to see if anyone was listening or could hear. Papa was there, in the corner of the living room, engrossed in reading the

newspaper, spectacles perched on the end of his nose. Sydney whispered into the phone. "Elliott, I think we should wait now. Until after we're married. I don't want to chance it. Again, that is. Once was enough of a risk." Sydney lowered her voice until it was barely audible. "We're just lucky we didn't get caught."
Elliott's voice sounded exasperated. "Well, I didn't mean we should do it again."

"What did you mean then?" she asked.

"We need to talk. You know—we have lots to plan and discuss, about the future, our future, together...and it's noisy at the Legion, with so many people and the music."

Sydney's spirits rose. "To start planning the wedding?"

"That's right," he said, perking up, breathing easier.

After she'd hung up, Sydney sat, phone clutched against the rising in her chest, and tried to quell the pounding in her heart.

Every evening after supper that week, she listened to love songs on the radio and dreamed the evenings away as she waited for Saturday to come.

I love everything about you.
your gentle good humor
your intellect
your shoes
your coat
your scarf
the way you move
the way you smile

River of Forgiveness

that connection when you understand
your brazenness
your nervousness
your kindness
your words
your mouth
your hands
the sweetness of your face
when you get happy and excited and emotional
I LOVE YOU

Chapter 5
Baptism, Communion and Confirmation

A few weeks later, Sydney and Helka went for a picnic at Current River, on their lunch break from the hospital laundry. Maisie had begun dating an intern from the nursing school. He was a few years older than she was. He'd been injured in the war and had a bit of a limp and a baby face with cheeks that seemed impossibly fat and puffy for his slender build. Sydney and Helka called him Chuffy. Maisie and Chuffy had gone for a walk along the river and Sydney spotted them, kissing under the cherry blossoms where they didn't think anyone could see.

Elliott was away and Sydney was restless and pent-up from missing him. She and Helka sat on a blanket, breathing in the scent of the flowers and the fresh air. The river here was fast with the spring thaw and filled the air with the sound of its rushing current. They spoke of their hopes for love and families of their own. They laughed at stories from the laundry and about Chuffy.

Helka flipped through the newspaper while they talked. "Listen to this," she said, reading from an article – **Babyface**, a story of a man who embezzled money from the bank where he worked. "Men with a baby face are three times less likely to be convicted of a criminal charge and three times more likely to be convicted of a white-collar crime," Helka read out to her. They laughed, thinking of Chuffy, his puffy red face, exhausted, exasperated at the hard, physical work, bleaching the sheets.

"Maisie had better watch out," Helka teased.

"Frenchie," Sydney heard someone call out. She turned to look, not believing her eyes.

"Spencer." He was standing over her with his boyish grin. Sydney leapt to her feet. "Oh Spence, it's so good to see you." She stood on her tiptoes and threw her arms around him, hugging him as hard as she could. "Welcome home." Spencer was with another soldier. They both wore their army uniforms and Spencer introduced him to Sydney and Helka.

Sydney said hello and then smiled in a motherly mocking way at Spencer and, pointing down to his hand, said, "and what's this?" Spencer was smoking a cigarette and, knowing him from the time he was a boy, Sydney thought it seemed so out of place.

"Ah, the army does that to you," he said.

Spencer looked grown up now. He was muscular and fit, his skin rough and masculine, and he wore stubble on his chin. They'd once stood almost eye to eye as children but he towered over her now, no longer the boy she knew, but for the unmistakable twinkle in his eye when he teased her.

Spencer held her back, appraising her. "Well, look at you. You've blossomed, Frenchie—you're a woman now and look at this—we're both in uniform." He held her hand and spun her around for a look, letting his hand linger on her wrist as he released her. They both laughed and Sydney flushed.

Spencer gently rubbed a thick finger along the bridge of her nose and Sydney felt him tremble a little. "Where are all your freckles?" he said.

"It's like a miracle. They've disappeared, just as Mum told me they would like hers did when she got older. They'll be back though when the sun comes out, I still get them on my nose." She grimaced. "But—the rest of my face? Gone," she said.

Spencer flipped open his wallet to show her he was still carrying around her school picture from their last year of high school together.

"Oh, Spencer, I can't believe you still have it," she said. Then, suddenly remembering, said, "I haven't seen you or told you—you won't believe it—Spencer, but, ta-da...drum roll. Wait for it. I've met someone." He looked suddenly sad and later that night Sydney thought of it, after she'd seen his face and wondered about it. Now though, she went on. "I've met someone truly special." Spencer held that same sullen expression on his face. She hadn't smiled or even felt flattered when he'd shown her the picture. She'd felt surprised, a little taken aback and a sudden memory of herself with Elliott, in his apartment, had made her blush with shame. Spencer seemed in a bit of a reverie as he held up the picture to show her and pronounced to her and Helka and the man who accompanied him that he'd always thought Sydney was one of the most attractive girls he knew; a justification, perhaps, for having kept the photograph in his wallet.

"Oh God, look at the time," Helka cried out, jumping up and folding their blanket. "We're late."

They said goodbye and ran back to the laundry as fast as they could. Sydney turned, to wave to Spencer. He stood, motionlessly, watching after her. "See you later, at the house," she said.

Sydney thought about Spencer for the rest of the afternoon, while she scrubbed the sheets. She thought back to when they were in their last year of high school. Sydney was only just an inch and a half over five feet, but her eyesight was good, greater than twenty/twenty, so she sat near the back of the class, where Spencer and the taller boys sat.

She and Spencer usually traded smiles every morning and spoke in low tones, catching up on their evenings or weekends. She never seemed to run into Spencer outside of class but every school day, there he was in his V-neck sweater and plaid shirt, his sandy hair combed straight and cut tidily, thick and parted at the side. When he laughed or teased her there was that twinkle in his bluish-grey eyes that she loved. When he wasn't smiling there was a seriousness there though, and Sydney thought, a bit of sadness. She wondered about it but it never seemed to affect Spencer's mood. He was calm and patient and he seemed kind.

It wasn't until close to the end of high school before Spencer left to go away in the army after they'd sat together, in the same class, year after year, exchanging cards at Christmastime, and traded a copy of each other's school pictures, that Sydney began to wonder how Spencer felt.

Afterward, on the way home from work at the laundry that day, Sydney was distracted and couldn't stop thinking about it. She wondered whether, through all the years of their friendship, Spencer had harbored special feelings for her. She had begun to see it was usually not at the parties one goes to or the dances at the church or Legion Hall, where you think you might meet someone new: those were not the moments that changed your life. It was usually moments such as that one with Spencer, moments you're caught off-guard when something shifts or changes and catches you from the other side, when a person you have known for a long time gives you cause to suddenly look at them in a different light. Unexpected moments, unanticipated events. Those were the times when ultimately one's life was defined. As it was the afternoon she'd walked in the door, home for lunch and there was Elliott Caldwell, sitting at her kitchen table.

Kiidumae

Sydney and Spencer seemed to keep running into one another everywhere after that day at Current River—on the way to the store, at the Wesley Street United Church, at the Legion Dances when Elliott was out of town travelling on business. Something had shifted, and Sydney intuitively knew she owned some part of Spencer. That there was a power she had over him she knew was always there as their friendship grew. Even after Spencer had gone away to the army for three years, that power was still there. Nothing had changed, but all of these thoughts were forgotten as soon as she saw Elliott Caldwell again.

Sydney's hands trembled as she fastened the top button on her white blouse after she got home that day. It was a little tight on her neck, by now being a few years old, graying a bit, revived by the strong bleach in the hospital laundry. On top of her blouse, she had first put on a red V-neck sweater, and then, at the last minute, switched it for more conservative emerald green. She pulled her grey and green plaid wool skirt up over a white slip. Then she rolled matching green tights up from the ankle to the top of her waist. Appraising herself, wanting to look pristine but not unfeminine, she placed her string of pearls under the collar of her blouse and clipped on the matching earrings. Brown eyeliner and red lipstick gave her the look of an alluringly innocent schoolgirl.

Perfect, she thought. *Now that I am to be Mrs. Elliott Edmond Caldwell, or "mrs. elliott edmond caldwell," as Elliott would write it, I don't want him or anyone else to think of me as loose. Elliott and I will just have to wait until after the wedding now.*

The walk, well, half-run, to Elliott's apartment, had settled most of the shakiness in her hands but it started again, a little, as she rang the buzzer to his apartment. The buzzer sounded four times before she began to fear he had forgotten she was coming. She checked her watch and realized she was almost fifteen minutes early. Then she heard Elliott's voice and was caught by the wildly exhilarating feeling it elicited in her.

"Sorry, Loves," Elliott called through the speaker, "nature calls."

Sydney pulled at the door quickly to open it before Elliott depressed the button code on the telephone to allow her access.

A blonde girl, who Sydney thought she recognized, passed her on the way out the door, head held down, averting eye contact with Sydney. An unpleasant feeling registered somewhere in the back of Sydney's mind as she tried to place the face. Betty. Betty Blackwell, a girl who'd been a few grades ahead of Sydney at the same school.

Elliott didn't look tidy and groomed that evening. His shirt was partially unbuttoned, and he wasn't wearing an undershirt as he usually did. He wore suspenders that drooped down over the top of his pants and his feet were bare. His hair was tousled.

"Hi, loves," he greeted her, kissing her first tenderly on each cheek, as he always did, then gently on her forehead. He stroked her hair back. "Oh Sydney, how I've missed you. A week is just too long to go without seeing you."

He pulled her toward him and he felt warm and had a manly scent about him. When his body was right against hers, she no longer cared about anything other than this moment. Without speaking, he was upon her, unbuttoning the neck of her white blouse, stroking her whenever her skin was exposed.

"I want to kiss you everywhere," Elliott said, into her ear.

Sydney's body tingled at the thought. Each time she saw him there seemed to be an exponential building of her feelings, her love of his hands and his fingers, his laugh, his intelligence, his toying precocious smile, his physical presence, all rolled into one large emanating feeling.

He began to kiss her. There was a taste of old tobacco smoke. She looked up at the cross hanging over Elliott's bed. Her sense of what was right told her there couldn't be anything wrong with this, that anything that felt so natural and real could not be wrong.

Elliott was still kissing her when he laid her down on the bed and pulled the emerald green cardigan and matching tights off, followed by her grey and green wool skirt until she lay beneath him with only her brassiere and pearl necklace. She felt the warmth of his body as he kissed around the perimeter of her brassiere and unfastened and removed it so easily and skillfully she hadn't even realized he'd done it. She was lost to the heat of their bodies and his kisses and, at once, the memory of Elliott dancing with Betty Blackwell at the Legion Hall returned to her. The two had been dancing together the night she and Elliott met. Sydney imagined Betty's desire for Elliott and this inflamed her desire even more as Elliott made love to her that evening.

Afterward, Sydney lay in bed, feeling warm, calm and relaxed. Elliott brought her a small sip of cherry brandy and she felt peaceful and content. He kissed her mouth then lit a cigarette. She stroked his chest, firm and smooth. She smiled. "I thought we were supposed to be planning our wedding tonight?"

She uncurled her legs from around his body and stretched out. It let out a squeak with her movement. "I hope we didn't make too much noise, with this old bed creaking."

"The neighbors will be envious," he smirked. He hesitated, "About the wedding…"

"Yes?" A little surge of fear shot through her.

"You know I'm a Catholic, right?"

"Well, of course, I know that. That's where you are every Sunday while I'm at the Wesley Street United Church."

"Yes, well, that's just it."

"What's just it?" she teased, her hand on his hip bone.

"I went to the diocese to ask."

"Ask what?"

"If I could marry you."

"Yes. What did they say, Elliott? Please tell me, what did they say?"

"The Catholic Church doesn't recognize a marriage unless both the bride and the groom are Catholic."

"So, what are you saying then?" She felt alarmed and choked back a sob.

He seemed irritable. "What I am saying, Sydney is that if we are to be married, you will need to convert to Catholicism."

She was silent for a while. "What does that mean then? I mean, Catholics and the United Church both believe in the same things, don't they? Jesus. The Old Testament. The New. What difference does it make? Can't we just get married in my church?"

"The difference, Sydney, is that my parents will never accept you. They wouldn't be happy if I married a non-Catholic."

Sydney went quiet. "Well, fine, I don't think it'll matter to my family, since we're both Christians." She was lost in thought for some time, then said, "So, let's do it. What do I have to do? How do I become a Catholic?"

Elliott looked pale. "You mean you would be willing to do it? You would actually go through with it?" His voice had a slight screech to it, as if in disbelief.

He caught himself then and said, "I mean, would you really do that? For me?"

She took his hand. For a moment he looked as though he might pull it away, then it came to rest. She looked into his eyes with tenderness. "Of course. Of course, I would." She spoke, quietly. "Just tell me what I need to do."

"It's a long process, Sydney. It's not as easy as it sounds. You need to go through the three stages," Elliott answered.

"What three stages?"

"Baptism. Communion. Confirmation."

"Baptism?" Sydney giggled. "Like a baby? Does it matter if I've already been baptized in the United Church? Does that count? Or do I have to wear a christening gown? Will I be getting a christening gown instead of a wedding gown?"

The thought of this made both of them laugh and Elliott held her close to him. He wrapped his arms around her and grazed his hand down her breast and along her side to her vagina.

"I think maybe you should go exactly like this," Elliott said. They fell asleep after that, worn out and languorous after their love-making. Sydney felt the graze of soft stubble on his face, against hers. A deep sense of familiar peace filled her that left her always wanting more.

Chapter 6
No Way Now, But Forward

"So, you're really going to go through with it then?" asked Helka. "You're actually going to become a Catholic?"

Sydney was sitting in the dark at the dining room table, still in her pajamas, receiver pressed close to her ear.

"Yes," she said. "Oh Helka, when I saw him that first time at our kitchen table, he seemed so steady and sure and I knew I wanted to be with him forever. There was just something about him."

"You've got it bad," said Helka.

"When you're in love, nothing else matters."

"Just don't lose yourself in the process," Helka warned—you should never love someone more than you love yourself; but I know you're hopeless already. So, do you get to ride in the golden chariot with the Pope now?" Helka giggled.

"No, I will not be riding in a chariot. I will be going through all the same rituals as any other Catholic does but I will find out more, for sure, when Elliott and I meet with the priest at St. Patrick's Cathedral this Sunday, after mass, my first mass. I will be sitting in a church pew next to my beloved fiancé, dreaming of having little Catholic babies running around everywhere. Lots of them too, since the Pope, it seems, does not approve of the diaphragm. All in good time, though. I don't even have an engagement ring yet. Elliott is working overtime, almost every week, to save up for one. That's why we only see each other on Saturday nights—for the dances at the Legion Hall," Sydney lied.

Helka bit her tongue. She and Allan Freeman, "two L'd Allan", as Sydney called him, the man she had just started dating, had been to the last two dances at the Legion and she knew Sydney had not been there. She'd surmised that she was with Elliott, at his apartment.

"Well, anyway, I'd like you to be my maid of honor Helka, at the wedding. Who would have ever guessed when we met in Grade Two that we'd be standing up for each other at our weddings?"

Helka fought back tears and laughed instead. "You got stuck in the mud in your new boots and I had to rescue you—you and that ridiculous pink snowsuit, with the bunny ears. The one Aunt Bessie sent you for Christmas. You got so hot you tried to pull it off. I had to help you when your cardigan got snagged in the zipper. Good thing Aunt Bess lived in Winnipeg and wasn't around to see the damage. And now, here I am, I'll be helping you into your long white gown a few months from now. Let's just make sure we don't get anything stuck in the zipper on that."

Sydney lifted Mum's white hand-crocheted tablecloth and knocked three times on the dining room table. "Knock on wood," she said. "Anyhow, I'll be doing the same for you Helka, when the time comes. We're not like old Francine Napier—we're not like those girls who have been falling in love every other week since Grade Eight."

"I know. I know," said Helka quietly.

"Sometimes it scares me. Sometimes I'm afraid of the power he has over me. Over my happiness, or unhappiness. Sometimes I feel like I wouldn't want to live without him."

Helka was silent. She remained silent for a long time.

"Well," said Sydney, finally. "I'd better go. I'll call you on Sunday, after my big meeting with the Pope, Ha, Ha."

"OK. Oh, and Sydney."

"Hmm?"

"You know that I love you? That we'll always be friends, no matter what happens."

"Yes, I know, Helka," she whispered. Sydney felt overwhelmed and was trying not to cry. "I knew that the first day—it was your feisty spirit when you were determined to unzip that hideous pink snowsuit, no matter what and ditto to you. You know I feel the same about you too, right? That I'll always want you for a friend, no matter what?"

"'Course I know, silly. You wouldn't have stuck around me and my weird parents all these years otherwise."

Sydney placed the receiver back on the wall in the dining room and stayed sitting in the chair in the dark for a long time. She felt a little scared, as if she were moving away from Helka in some indefinable way. That the place that had been their friendship all these years would soon become something else, part of it replaced by Elliott Caldwell, but she knew there was no way now but forward.

Chapter 7
Chuffy

It was Maisie, of all people, quiet, shy Maisie who proved to be the one to push the issue of marriage and matrimony and the timing of Sydney's wedding. She came home one night after working all day at the laundry then out on a date to a movie, *Gentleman's Agreement,* starring Gregory Peck, and afterward for a soda at the Ice Cream Store on Main Street with Chuffy. Chuffy, the intern she'd been dating for a time, happened also to be the boss's son down at the laundry and his father had just promoted him to supervisor. He and Maisie had been celebrating that night. *He is as shy and quiet as Maisie but, at least, Maisie has her beauty*, Sydney thought, *with her near jet-black hair and blue eyes—such an unusual combination. Maisie's wardrobe of blue plaid skirts with royal blue sweaters highlights the blue of her eyes and the shape of her body.*

'But Chuffy was plain as the day is long,' Mum always said.

"Ugh," said Deedee. "It's just disgusting. I can't believe Maisie is going to marry that chump. The last time I saw him, I walked in on him and Maisie on the veranda. Mum and Papa were sitting outside with the neighbors, enjoying the hot night, and there he was, his cane lying on the floor beside him, huffing and puffing all over Maisie, pants down, and I could see the white of his rear-end glowing under the moonlight. There's no way I'm ever letting any boy do that to me, not before I'm married, anyway. Not before I've got the ring on my finger. All's bony old Chuffy is saying now, smiling away as the cat who swallowed the canary, strutting around the laundry, bragging right in front of everybody, Maisie said— 'well, I've done it. I've got myself an Archambault girl,' like we were some kind of trophy or something."

Sydney took all of this in. She had been so preoccupied with Elliott Caldwell and work at the laundry and classes at St. Patrick's Cathedral she hadn't even noticed Maisie, lately.

"Congratulations," she said to Maisie later, when they were sitting in the living room with Mum and Papa. Sydney got up and gently squeezed Maisie's upper arm. "I'm so happy for you, Maisie, truly I am."

River of Forgiveness

In truth though, Sydney was feeling a little off-center. She was the eldest. She was the one who had met someone first. She was the first to be engaged. She was the one who should be getting married first.

"There's more," Maisie said, with a shy, triumphant smile, her hands folded in the middle of her neat plaid skirt. "I'm having a baby," Maisie said softly, but her happiness bubbled underneath. "Well, not just me, Chuffy and I, we're going to have a baby. So we're going to have the wedding right away. Just down at City Hall, with my friend Francine Napier standing up for me and Chuffy's brother standing up for him."

Mum gave a painful sounding groan, as though someone had just wounded her but 'what was done was done' she lamented and, at least there was a wedding to follow soon so there was nothing more to be said. Accept the cards as laid and start to plan the wedding. What will be, will be. Since the war had ended, Mum seemed to have softened.

Papa was silent but looked relieved not to have to intervene—he'd been worried when Maisie had asked them all to come and sit down in the living room. "Well, nobody's died then," he said and shuffled back to his game of solitaire spread out on the dining room table, at his usual spot.

"Wait," Sydney called out, not to be outdone in this way by her younger sister. "I have news, too," she announced.

Papa shuffled back to the living room and sat next to Mum, glancing at her warily and giving out a little sigh.

"Not both of you?" cried Mum. "Didn't I teach you girl's anything?"

"Oh, no Mum, it's nothing like that," Sydney said.

"Well, look how I trusted Maisie," Mum said. She coughed and looked away, tears brimming in her eyes.

Sydney wished she could take it back then as she caught Maisie's scornful look in her direction. For a moment, Maisie looked as though she might flee from the room in tears but she stayed seated rigidly in the armchair, hands clasped lovingly over her belly. Like it or not, she wanted to hear Sydney's news.

Deedee gave a knowing little smirk.

"Elliott Caldwell has proposed to me." Sydney halted. There was silence in the room. "And I have accepted."

Neither Mum nor Papa spoke for a few moments.

"Well, aren't you going to say anything? Aren't you happy for me? All this excitement about Maisie and now no one seems to care about me." Sydney scowled.

"Don't be silly. Of course, we're happy for you," Mum said. "It's just that, it's just—"

"What?" Sydney asked. "It's just what? You don't like him, is that it?" Sydney's face flushed red and she jumped up from her chair, demanding an answer. She was surprised at her own defensiveness.

"Why no, that's not it at all, dear. We hardly know him. So, I can't say as I don't like him. No, it's not that."

"Well, what then?" Sydney was getting exasperated.

"It's just I always thought, well, we always thought—your father and I—that you would marry Spencer. That's all." Mum spoke softly. Sydney saw her eyes glisten with a few tears. She looked a little shaky. "You and Spencer have been friends since grade school. The best of friends."

Sydney was so taken aback she wasn't sure what to say, at first. "That's the whole point, Mum," she said finally—Spencer and I are the best of friends. Just friends—but one doesn't marry a friend. Mum, I know how much you like Spencer but I'm not in love with Spencer." She had not thought this would be so difficult. "I am in love with Elliott Caldwell."

Mum looked over at Papa. "Well," she said, resigned, "look at your father and I—ten years apart is the perfect age for a marriage—enough of a difference that a man won't need to wander."

Papa cleared his throat and looked down at his lap. Maisie and Deedee suppressed a giggle.

"Yeah, but you'll be an early widow—don't women live ten years longer than men?" Deedee asked.

Mum threw a warning look in Deedee's direction and said, "Well, then Sydney dear, we will give you our support. You know what's best for yourself. You have always shown good judgment and if Elliott Caldwell is the man you feel will make you happy then that is all that matters to us."

"Yes, Mum, he is." Sydney spoke resolutely. She hesitated before continuing then decided she may as well finish this, get it over with, once and for all.

"There's more—I, I'm converting to Catholicism. That's how much I want to marry him."

Mum gave out a little cry and swatted at the air in front of her, as though she'd been stung by a bee. She stretched out an arm for her iodine bottle, never far from her reach, and dabbed it over her throat, to quell her rising blood pressure. "Oh, my," she said. "This has all been just a little too much."

That night, as Sydney lay in her bed across from Deedee's, she thought over everything that had happened and been said in the living room. She gloated over her news, even though she felt a little guilty about trumping Maisie's. She glowed about having made it real. Now that she had told Mum and Papa, it solidified things. It seemed as though it was now going to happen. She fretted a bit over what Elliott would say when she told him her parents knew and so they would now have to set a date but mostly she thought about how she had felt when her mother had mentioned Spencer and when Mum commented on the importance of her happiness.

Sydney had not considered her decision or her love for Elliott Caldwell in the context of happiness or unhappiness. In fact, other than the times she felt secure in Elliott's arms, during their lovemaking, her relationship with him had mostly seemed to be comprised of angst and feelings of insecurity. She did not appreciate the way he treated her at times. She did not care for the way he had spoken to her in such an offhand, flippant manner at his apartment the other day but she did know that she was very much in love with him.

Spencer, on the other hand, was uncomplicated. She always felt happy when she was with him. They talked and laughed and teased and knew each other so well they were comfortable not speaking, just being in one another's company, ambling along the walkway at Current River, licking their ice cream cones, window shopping on Main Street after the stores closed, talking about the items they saw in the windows that they thought were hideous or would like to buy someday.

Sydney found herself aching for that simplicity again. In a way, she wanted her old self back. She missed who she had been before Elliott Caldwell had claimed her but time with Spencer was a little dull. There was always a sense of it not being enough; that this was all there was and all there ever would be. There was none of that feeling of unknown, indescribable magic in life that Sydney had not yet experienced. This is how she always felt when she was with Elliott, the feeling that her life was only just beginning.

Chapter 8
Let's Talk About the Wedding

"Will you always have to be travelling so much?" Sydney asked Elliott, as she ran her fingers through his dark chest hair. "After we're married, I mean."

Elliott sat himself up and pulled Sydney toward him. He lay her back down on the bed with her head on the pillow and kissed her deeply on the mouth. "It's only for a while, until I get myself built up."

"What do you mean?" She laughed and nuzzled her chin under his. "Built up to what?" She took a sip from her glass of cherry brandy and lifted it to toast her fiancé.

Kiidumae

"Oh, you jest now but just you wait and see—'only cream and bastards rise to the top'—and I, my darling, plan to be the '*crème de la crème*'. I plan to have at least forty men under me," Elliott boasted. "Maybe even franchise it out the same as the Ben Franklin stores. That way," he said and tickled her ribs, "you and I can just spend all day, right here, alone together. We can listen to Chopin and read to each other."

Elliott picked up the e.e. cummings book Sydney had given him for Christmas. He thumbed through it.

"Ah-ha. Here you go, loves. I've found the perfect poem for you:

your homecoming will be my homecoming--

my selves go with you,only i remain;
a shadow phantom effigy or seeming

(an almost someone always who's noone)

a noone who,till their and your returning,
spends the forever of his loneliness
dreaming their eyes have opened to your morning

feeling their stars have risen through your skies:

so,in how merciful love's own name,linger
no more than selfless i can quite endure
the absence of that moment when a stranger
takes in his arms my very life who's your

—when all fears hopes beliefs doubts disappear. Everywhere and joy's perfect wholeness we're

"OK? You get the picture?" Elliott said, smiling.

"Perfectly," Sydney said, "except what does effigy mean?"

"It means a likeness. An image."

She felt a sinking feeling in her stomach. Something about his bravado didn't ring true. It felt false. Maybe even a little irrational.

Elliott giggled with a high-pitched squeak. Sydney thought he seemed nervous or uncomfortable, as though he wanted to get away from this thin ice they were skating on.

"Seriously though," she said, faltering. She felt as if she might tear up. "You're away for days, weeks, at a time."

Elliott thought for a moment, as though trying to come up with an answer to appease her, to avoid a scene.

"You can always come with me," he said. "We can travel the road, together, you and me, a regular Bonnie and Clyde."

"Except, hopefully, we won't be robbing any banks," Sydney sighed. She just didn't seem to ever be able to get a straight answer from him whenever the subject of seriously planning their life came about.

Elliott had a look of concern on his face as he studied Sydney's, perceiving her doubts. "Well, first things first, Loves," he said. Let's start by deciding on a date for the wedding."

She perked up and sat straight against her pillow. "Really?" Sydney squealed with delight. "Oh, yes, let's. Oh, Elliott, you are always right. Yes, let's decide on a date right now. When do you think would be the best time? For your business, I mean."

"The middle of winter, Christmas Day, is likely my slowest time," he teased.

"Forget that, Elliott Edmond Caldwell. I'm not wearing pom-poms and fur-lined boots on my wedding day. C'mon now. When is your slow time, when the weather is nice?"

"It all depends on what business I happen to line up," he said, with a wink, "but I suppose if you were to say there was a slow time, it is likely on the long weekends when everyone is out of town. Here, let me get the calendar."

He lifted his calendar off the night table and flipped the pages over quickly, as though there was something he didn't want Sydney to see. He settled on May, where there was a picture of a boat in Port Arthur Harbor.

"How about the twenty-fourth of May? We can sail away together, on the Good Ship *Queen of Cheshire*," Elliott teased. He'd been teaching her how to play chess, his favorite board game, and had started calling her that. "Anyone coming from out of town will have more travel time."

"Sounds perfect," Sydney cooed.

"Done," he said. "Your wish is my command, me lady." He hopped out of bed and stood next to her, with the top sheet wrapped around his waist as he held it together with his hand. He bowed down and kissed her foot, as she sat cross-legged against the pillow, and she folded it beneath her, similar to a little bird.

"Shall I peel you a grape, my soon-to-be-Madame?" Elliott said.

"Ah, silly you," she laughed. Her eyes filled with tears. She had never felt so happy. "OK now, who should we invite?" Sydney asked. "Let's get a piece of paper and make a list."

She made up the list and came to a total of almost two hundred people—most of them her family and friends and relatives. Other than his parents, Elliot had mumbled the name of one friend, and a few aunts and uncles, after she persisted.

"Of course, I'll have to write home to England, to ask," he said, "but I'm sure they'll all be delighted and Mum and Dad wouldn't miss it for the world."

"It's going to be pretty empty over on your side of the church," Sydney said. "Maybe we'll just mix everybody up with the seating, have both sides sitting together."

"That's brilliant," he said. She wasn't sure if he was being sarcastic and, although she hated to admit it, he sounded rather disinterested.

"What?" Elliott asked her when he noticed her scowl. "Weddings are for women, Loves. And for other people. If it was up to us men, we would just have a simple ceremony with two people." Sydney was still pouting. "I just want you to be happy, Loves, so have it whatever way you want."

Kiidumae

She looked up at him, relenting. He could tell she was coming around. "C'mon now," Elliott said, pulling her back down on the bed and tugging the sheet out from under her and up over their heads.

"Let's start the honeymoon early."

"Again?" she teased, and they both laughed and slid down under the sheets.

Later, when Sydney went to leave, it started to rain. Elliott walked her home, throwing his grey trench coat over his suit pants and slipping into his shoes, without socks. He put his arm around her and held her body into his, close, so they could share his umbrella. Their bodies were relieved of all tension. It was a warm rain and so, when the umbrella jostled back and forth and the rain dampened their faces, they let themselves get wet. They were both smiling and silent.

By the time they reached the sidewalk leading to her front porch, Sydney's hair was soaked, and rain slid down her curls into her eyes and onto the brim of her lip and chin. Elliott kissed her goodbye, passionately, and the raindrops merged inside their mouths like a warm wash.

Chapter 9
Papa Puts His Foot Down

After hearing Sydney and Maisie's news, Mum was shaken and blamed herself. "Where did I go wrong?" she said. "I'm a failure as a mother."

The daily bible readings were reinstituted, with only Sydney and Deedee now since Maisie had moved into a tiny box of a house over on Onion Road with Chuffy, given to them by Chuffy's father as a wedding present.

Mum hovered over Deedee now too, nagging at her, questioning her whenever she went anywhere, determined she wasn't going to fall into the same fate as Sydney and Maisie.

Kiidumae

"You're going to turn the girl into a nervous wreck," Papa said, scolding Mum. He took to having Deedee meet him at the shipyard for a few hours each day after school and kept her busy fastening on rivets, so he could keep an eye on her; get her away from Mum for a bit.

The strain of it all caused Mum's rheumatic fever to flare, and it tired her. She took to her bed most afternoons after lunch, when all her chores were done. Deedee brought books home for her from the school library—books like *Wuthering Heights* and *Jane Eyre*—and Mum locked herself in her room, reading and sleeping.

She nagged at Papa now too, even more than she used to, blaming him for not being strict enough with the girls. "It's time to drag yourself away from those interminable games of cards and do something," she said. "I can't do it all myself."

Papa went out into the backyard and built a rink where the pond pooled in the springtime. He borrowed a pair of skates from one of Sydney's friends and taught Deedee to ice skate. He wasn't hard on Deedee, because the poor girl had done nothing wrong; he only wanted to look after her.

He was determined, though, to keep a tighter rein on Sydney, until she was married and living on her own then Mum would stop fretting so.

One Saturday Elliott asked Sydney if she could meet him at his apartment instead of him meeting her at her front gate. He said he had a late appointment, installing a door viewer in the home of a recently widowed woman who worked at the

River of Forgiveness

Bioped Footcare Center on Saturdays until 6 o'clock, and then the woman had to close up the store but Sydney surmised that Elliott was also avoiding her parents. The last time he'd come to meet her, he'd turned his head toward the street as he waited, avoiding any eye contact that would require him to say hello. The guilt. She was learning already how the Catholic Church infused that. Guilty of their lie about being at the Legion Dances. Guilty of making love every week when they met now when they were not yet married. Papa scowled when Sydney headed out the door unescorted.

"What kind of a gentleman is he?" Papa griped.

Sydney defended Elliott. "Oh Papa, but it's beginning to get lighter outside now and he has to work late. I don't mind the walk on my own," she emphasized.

She flushed a little hot though after realizing how convincingly she'd said it. How easy it had been to believe it—to lie to her own father.

"Wait there Sydney, while I get my coat. I'm coming with you."

"What?" she almost screamed. "I mean, what for Papa? This is not at all necessary."

"In my day, Sydney, young ladies did not go gallivanting on their own to the Legion Hall."

"But I used to go on my own all the time, Papa before I met Elliott."

"That was different. You went with Helka then."

"Oh, all right," Sydney relented.

Kiidumae

She knew there was no point in arguing with Papa when he got this way and she knew there must be more to it than that. She wondered if he suspected.

Sydney was silent on the walk to the Legion Hall. She found herself hoping Papa would not take this any further and insist on coming inside; then he'd see Elliott wasn't there. She gnawed on the inside of her cheek and bit at her nails. Elliott would be wondering where she was; she was never late and she hoped he wouldn't go to their house. She suddenly felt the web of her duplicity and was ashamed. It hadn't seemed to matter when no one knew—when no one was any the wiser.

"Well, here we are," Papa said.

Sydney was relieved when she looked up and saw Helka standing on the steps waiting—likely for two L'd Allan, watching as she and Papa walked down the street toward the Legion Hall. Sydney caught Helka's eye and motioned behind Papa's back for her to keep silent.

"Oh, Helka," Papa said, sounding relieved. "Hello."

"Good evening Mr. Archambault."

"It's about time," Helka scolded Sydney, as if on cue.

"It's my fault, Helka," Papa said, a little sheepishly. "I held her up, waiting for me. You girls go on and have a good time then." He kissed Sydney lightly on the cheek and told her to be home by twelve.

"Yes, Papa." She smiled and blew her father a kiss.

"What's going on?" asked Helka.

Sydney explained it all then told Helka she had to hurry, or Elliott would wonder where she was and start to worry.

"Well, it wouldn't hurt for you to play just slightly hard-to-get every once in a while," Helka chided.

"Ah, Helka," Sydney said and squeezed her arm. "Thanks for covering for me. You are the best." She ran off toward Elliott's apartment.

Chapter 10
Cheshire Queen

Sydney spotted e.e. cummings name while wandering through the book store shortly before their first Christmas together. Everything that e.e. cummings had ever written, Elliott Caldwell read and collected. He told her that everyone said he looked just like e.e., at least he did when he was younger and, because of that, he had become a fastidious, almost obsessive reader of his books, burying into them daily from the dog-eared collection he carried with him in his suitcase when he was on the road. Elliott signed his name in lower case too, in deference to e.e. Sydney often wondered what that said about him.

At the front of the book store, there were a few tables piled high with games. Sydney shuffled through the boxes of Chinese Checkers, Scrabble, Cribbage—all the games Papa had taught her to play that she and Elliott now played on Sunday afternoons after mass. Then she saw it. The chess set. All the hand-carved pieces were set up on a little table, ready to play.

On Christmas Eve, after he'd opened his new chess set, Sydney listened to Chopin's music and watched Elliott, sitting next to her on the bed, naked, a sheet wrapped around his groin, the dark hairs of his long legs stretched out in front of him as he leaned back on the pillows. She sat next to him on her side of the bed, naked also, bathed in just enough light from the lamp to illuminate the pawns and rooks and knights and bishops. Elliott said he was the King and she was the Queen. The air was a little cool and made her nipples erect, as she sat on the edge of the bed, a sheet draped across the middle of her body.

"My Cheshire cat," Elliott said. "Queen Cheshire."

She was conscious of Elliott's eyes on her throughout the game with each move she made, and a slow kind of erotic sensation flushed her cheeks. By the time Elliott called "checkmate," a passion she had never known she was capable of had overtaken her.

Elliott reached for her through a space they had both silently cleared and he wrapped his arms around her. He kissed her hard and caressed her as he kicked the board onto the floor and laid her beneath him.

"Still the reigning King," Sydney teased him afterward, as he lay propped above her, stroking the soft stubble on his chin, 'King e.e. caldwell.'"

"I kind of like that," Elliott said, stroking her chin softly, in the same spot as she was stroking his.

On that first Christmas, Elliott gave Sydney a green leather diary and a small box that contained what she thought were diamond earrings. Later, she was to learn they were high-leaded glass, a cheap manmade stone that looks like a diamond. Elliott had not corrected her when she'd opened them and, by the time she found out, Sydney hadn't cared anyway. She loved them. They had come from him and they looked real. She knew he was saving for their wedding.

Elliott loved his new chess set. He talked about his grandfather and how they'd always played chess together while his mother cooked the Christmas turkey and his father read whatever book he had received in his stocking, alternating peeks at the chessboard as the game progressed, biting his tongue so as not to correct Elliott's moves.

In addition to the chess game, Sydney bought Elliott the sheet music with the original score of the *Nocturne*. It was hard for Sydney to fathom that the squiggle of notes was a language that kept hidden such beautiful music. She also bought him two books—Arthur Hedley's biography *Chopin* and one of e.e.'s books of poetry Elliott wanted for his collection. After he'd opened it she inscribed the front page of *Chopin*–"For my beautiful, naked Maestro, this book comes with undying love from your ever faithful Cheshire Queen," and inside the

cover of e.e. cummings book, one of his poems—to
e.e. caldwell, alias e.e., cummings:

i like my body when it is with your
body.   It is so quite new a thing.
Muscles better and nerves more.
i like your body.   i like what it does,
i like its hows.   i like to feel the spine
of your body and its bones,and the trembling
-firm-smooth ness and which i will
again and again and again
kiss,   i like kissing this and that of you,
i like, slowly stroking the,shocking fuzz
of your electric fur,and what-is-it comes
over parting flesh….And eyes big love-crumbs,

and possibly i like the thrill

of under me you so quite new

  Elliott had loved them both so much; it was the first and only time she had seen him overcome with emotion.
  "Oh Syd," he'd said, "I'm not worthy. I am not at all deserving of you." He poured her a little glass of cherry brandy and kissed her cheek. "We are, both of us, you and I, ill-fated to become a couple of voluptuaries—people devoted to luxury and sensuous pleasure—I'm afraid."
  Later, Sydney would recall those words and understand their true meaning.

River of Forgiveness

That same Christmas, Helka met Will Kirby at the Legion dance on New Year's Eve. He was the man she knew she'd marry within a half-hour of meeting him, she told Sydney that night.

"Sydney, I now know how you feel. You were right, I knew almost as soon as I met him."

"Maybe we can have a double wedding. Tell me what happened—when you met, how it all fell into place, how you knew. Oh, Helka dear, do tell me everything."

Helka went silent for a few moments.

"Ah, come on Helka, Don't be coy. Give me the goods. Just tell me what happened. Moment by moment."

"It was in the line-up at the washroom door of all places. Will was in line for the men's and I was in line for the ladies. So we ended up side by side for a few minutes as we made our way toward the washroom doors. He said I looked familiar. I thought it was just a line but he's a doctor at the hospital. I guess he saw me in the hallway or the cafeteria.

"'I was hoping to have an opportunity to introduce myself to you,'" he said. He seemed a little shy and a bit nervous. I told him my name then the men's line-up was moving much faster than the ladies so he asked if it was all right if he came and joined me at my table for a while, and of course, I said yes."

"How romantic," said Sydney, "just like a dream."

"Yes," Helka said. "It was. He came and sat down and we talked about everything under the sun and about his medical practice. He's a general practitioner but he delivers babies at the hospital and that got us talking about how much we both loved children. He said he wanted lots of them, maybe five, and I laughed and said I'd always thought five was the perfect number. He laughed at that then he asked me to dance. We went up on the floor, it was a slow dance, Claude Thornhill and His Orchestra, with Fran Warren, singing *A Sunday Kind of Love*, my absolute favorite song, and I could feel his hand tremble a little when he touched the small of my back. Oh Sydney, I just wanted to protect him. Right there I wanted to put my hand on his arm to quell his nervousness, I wanted to link my arm through his and walk with him to wherever he was going. I felt both protective of him and protected by him." Helka stopped for a while, lost in these thoughts.

Sydney swallowed hard. Somehow this was all making her Saturday night trysts with Elliott Caldwell seem seedy in comparison. She had missed the New Year's Eve Dance at the Legion to be with Elliott—again. All this lying to her parents made her feel queasy with guilt and she no longer liked herself until she got to Elliott's apartment then her body would go limp and all thought, reason and restraint no longer seemed possible.

"Oh Sydney, the way Will looked at me after the dance. His eyes were soft and kind. He held me very close, just for a moment, and said 'Helka, I hope you don't mind but I think I may be falling in love with you.' I was startled to hear him say this so quickly but then he said, 'I know it's soon but I've been noticing you for some while, at a distance, around the hospital and at the Legion Dances.' I couldn't believe I had never noticed him before. He's a little on the shorter side, just maybe four inches or so taller than me, with almost black hair, and he wears dark-rimmed glasses. So, from a distance, he isn't a man you would take notice of, particularly. Not like Elliott Caldwell," Helka said shyly. "He's not a looker like Elliott—not a man that all the ladies notice. Well, you know what I mean, Sydney; but when I get close to him something about his depth, his intensity, his sensitivity and warmth, draw me close. He's fun, too. We have lots of laughs."

Sydney took all this in after Helka hung up the phone. Since grade school, she had always had Helka to herself. Helka wasn't a real looker either, a little gangly, slightly boyish, with a shaggy head of naturally curly dirty blonde hair, a thick square-ish face and grey-blue eyes but she was full of energy. She was smart and fun too, as she had said Will was. Somehow, Sydney had never counted on having to share Helka but it was more than that. It wasn't losing part of Helka that bothered her so much about their conversation. It was that during Helka's recounting of her meeting of Will Kirby it had dawned on Sydney that Elliott Caldwell had never said he loved her. He'd never really told her how he felt about her. He liked her body, physically, she knew that, and he did say they should get married but something about Helka's story of falling in love rang true. It seemed real. A shadow of doubt edged its way through Sydney's consciousness and landed itself in the creases of her furrowed brow. When it had planted itself there, it would not seem to go away.

She was unable to quell the feeling of uneasiness that was now firmly embedded there.

Of whether or not she loved Elliott Caldwell, Sydney had no doubt. Admittedly, she did not know him well and realized she wasn't discovering much new about him at each subsequent meeting at his apartment. It was always the same—talk of the music, whatever books he was reading, games of chess before they made love. Today, she determined she would find out more, would find out why. She was solaced with the knowledge he had asked her to convert to Catholicism, even though he had been unable to attend most of the sessions because of work travel and commitments.

Chapter 11
Je t'aime

On New Year's Day, Sydney ordered a Grasshopper Cocktail made with green Crème de Menthe liqueur, as she always did when she went to the Cascades for lunch. It was nicer during the day because you could see the Falls better. She had taken Elliott there, to see the Falls—Kakabeka Falls.

He came to pick her up in his 1945 burgundy Buick he used for work and they'd driven up together for the day. There was a lot of snow piled on the side of the road, steep banks, but the roads were clear and it had been a crisp sunny day. Elliott turned the radio on to the classical station and cranked up Wagner's *Ride of the Valkyries*, singing out the melody, waving one hand through the air, the other hand firmly groping the wheel. Sydney held her left hand on his knee and laughed. Everything felt so warm when she was with Elliott but things had also begun to feel a little surreal as if something were slipping away, something she was unable to see.

Sydney had only just taken the first sip of her drink. Elliott took a fast gulp of his vodka and motioned to the waitress with his finger to bring him another, averting Sydney's gaze at the same time.

"Elliott," Sydney said softly, looking down at her glass.

"Why so serious?" he asked, smiling as he looked around the restaurant uneasily.

"Well, you'll never guess," she said, feigning a breezy air.

"What? Tell me."

Elliott held her chin with his fingers and tipped her face up toward his.

"It's Helka. She's met someone special."

"Well, that's wonderful then, Loves," he said with an air of relief. He visibly relaxed and loosened his tie a little. He looked handsome with his face flushed, shirt open at the collar. "That's good then, isn't it? Why so grave? Is it someone you don't like?"

"Oh, no. Nothing like that. I actually haven't even been introduced to him yet. Helka only just met him last night. She was with him, at the Legion New Year's Eve dance."

Sydney felt a little sad at that and her face fell. She wished she could have been there. She missed her old self sometimes, the days when it was just her and Helka.

"She called this morning to tell me."

"Oh, well, that sounds like good news. She must be very happy then. Don't' get me wrong Syd, Helka is a nice enough person but she's a little dull-looking."

Sydney's face flushed hot with a streak of rage. She felt protective of Helka.

"Well, looks aren't everything then, I guess," she pronounced, because this fellow Helka met, Dr. Will Kirby, Sydney emphasized, has already said he is falling in love with her."

Sydney was feeling a rush of emotions, anger, resentment, jealousy over Helka, sudden disappointment in Elliott Caldwell.

"Well, now, that seems a little fast, doesn't it?" Elliott asked. "I mean if they've only had one date."

Sydney calmed at the reasonableness of this statement.

"Yes, I suppose it is, a little," she agreed, "but he's been noticing her from afar for a while now, he told Helka. He's seen her around the hospital."

Sydney smiled a little, pleased to be able to come to Helka's defense.

"A doctor then, is he? A good catch for a girl like Helka, to be sure," Elliott said, his face squirming up into a look of distaste that made Sydney want to smack him. She thought she detected a glimpse of jealousy.

"Yes, he is," Sydney agreed, defensively, "but that's not the point, anyway. The actual point here is—"

"Yes, well, tell me, please, just exactly what is the point?" Elliott snapped, condescendingly.

Sydney felt a flash of anger at his chauvinism.

"The point here, Elliott," she emphasized, "the point here is you and me."

"How do you mean?" Elliott asked. "What has this to do with you and me?"

"Well, here we are, you and I, engaged to be married, and…"

"Yes? What of it?"

"Well, doesn't it seem odd to you that, here you and I are soon to be married and I don't think you've even once said you loved me," Sydney blurted out? To her horror, her eyes stung with tears. "I hadn't noticed it before. It hadn't dawned on me until this morning when Helka told me about Will Kirby."

Elliott didn't say anything for what seemed to be an overly long time.

"Of course I do, if I didn't then we wouldn't be getting married now, would we? Would I have said I wanted to marry you if I didn't?"

Sydney softened momentarily at his tone then flared up again. "Didn't what?" she commanded. "See. You can't even say it now."

"Now, I think you are getting a little hysterical here over nothing. You're sounding rather…"

"Rather what?" she demanded.

"You're sounding rather paranoid."

"Paranoid," Sydney shrieked. "This is my life we're talking about here."

"You're starting to make a scene. I think we'd better go back to the car," Elliott scolded, as though she were a child. "Shouldn't you have better asked me something this private when we were alone together?"

The waiter set two bowls of clam chowder in front of them then brought a basket of crusty rolls. Elliott threw a dollar bill down on their table and stood up to go. Without looking back at Sydney, he stormed out of the restaurant and back to the car.

Sydney was afraid he'd drive off without her but he sat with the car idling, cradling his head in his hands and running his fingers through his dark hair hanging down in his eyes as he leaned forward.

She had never seen him angry before and she felt a mixture of fear and tension and desire rise up within her. She got in the car beside him and placed a hand on his shoulder. He didn't move. They sat that way, together, for a while, and Sydney wished she had never brought it up in the first place.

"I'm sorry, Elliott. I'm so sorry for ruining our day. You're right. Nothing matters except you and me. Nothing matters other than we are together." She started to cry. "All that matters is that soon we will be married."

Elliott sighed and put an arm around Sydney's shoulders and swept away her tears. He pulled a Kleenex from the box on the dashboard and gently touched at the corners of her eyes.

"Love is not what you say," he whispered. "Love is what you do." He pulled her toward him and held her. He kissed her forehead. "*J't'aime*," he said quietly. "*J't'aime, mon Cherie*, I wish you could learn to trust me."

Sydney promised herself she would not ask again or push him to say something that did not come naturally to him. She reasoned he must be a man who is uncomfortable expressing his emotions. Mum was always telling her this about Papa but this new feeling was a fear she hadn't known before. Sometimes it felt as though time and life had stood still and Sydney held her breath waiting, as though something was going to happen, something over which she no longer had any control.

On the drive back to Port Arthur, Elliott shut the radio off. It was snowing lightly, wet snow that landed softly on the windshield and turned instantly to water, the slap, slap, of the wipers clearing it as quickly as it fell. Sydney had lost her desire to talk about their wedding plans. All she wanted was to go home.

Elliott dropped her off at her house and she got out of the car sulkily. She went directly to her room and lay down on the bed. She felt exhausted and emotionally drained but within a few hours, she was filled with remorse and wanted only to be with Elliott again. To have him convince her everything was all right. She fell into a deep sleep and dreamed he was kissing her then with her face buried in his neck against his, heard him whisper '*Je t'aime*.' She awoke to a loud knock on the door. It was Mum.

"Sydney, Elliott Caldwell is on the phone. He said he urgently needs to speak to you," Mum said, disapprovingly.

Chapter 12
The Way the River Flows

"Tell me, Spence," Sydney said, "why is it again the river flows back to the ocean?" They were sitting side by side on Spencer's Hudson's Bay picnic blanket at Current River, watching the waves churn over the stones, birds chirping in the tree branches above. It was mid-May, and a week to the day before her wedding.

"All those books you read, Frenchie, and you don't even know that?" He winked at her.

"I know, I know," she said, exasperated with herself. "We learned it in school but I can never seem to remember, all those tributaries and everything."

Kiidumae

It was the first time Sydney and Spencer had been alone together since he'd come back from the war. Mum was having a big wedding shower for her that afternoon and Aunt Bess had shipped one of her gifts ahead of time—a family heirloom. It was the big old oak chair she used to sit cross-legged on with Uncle Thierry in their living room while they listened to music when she'd lived with them. She'd forgotten about the chair when she returned home but he had fond memories of her perched there, Aunt Bess said and wanted her to have it.

Spencer had just bought himself a brand-new red Ford pick-up truck and offered to take her to Greyhound Shipping to pick it up. She wanted to sit in the chair for her shower. She was a little disappointed when she peeked inside the box and saw that Uncle Thierry had painted it a creamy color for her wedding. It was a thoughtful gesture—he, likely thinking a woman would want it to look pretty and feminine. What she'd loved most about it as a child though, was the look and feel of the beautiful grainy dark wood, the texture. Still, she'd been touched by the sentiment and at the idea of having the chair to cherish in her new home with Elliott.

After they'd picked it up, Spencer took her for a spin to show off his new truck. They flew down the highway, country music blaring on the radio, hair blowing in with the wind through the open windows. The air was alive with the scent of dust and fresh spring blossoms. She was giddy with the freedom of youth. Afterward, he brought her to sit by the river. Elliott was away, travelling on business and Sydney wouldn't be seeing him until their wedding day, at the church.

He'd called her that night—on New Year's Day—after they'd been to the Cascades when she'd wanted him to say "I love you," and he'd vowed then he would show her how much he did. He booked a honeymoon trip for them by train, to Niagara Falls in New York. Kakabeka Falls had inspired him, he said. "It's the Honeymoon Capital of the World, Loves, and the falls, of course, are the *piece de resistance*." Afterward, they were going to come back through Niagara-on-the-Lake, where they would dine and visit the theatre and art shops.

Last week, before he headed out on the road, he'd called to say they must not see each other again before the wedding, or it would be bad luck. He told her he wanted his first sight on their wedding day to be of her, standing at the altar, dressed in white, waiting for him.

Spencer hadn't come to the house or even telephoned to congratulate Sydney last fall after he'd heard the news of her impending marriage. He'd quit the army soon after he returned to Port Arthur and now that the war was over, he'd gone back to civilian life. He got a job down at the grain elevator, hucking sacks for shipment. The grain weighed up to sixty pounds a bushel and Spencer, already in top shape from his stint in the army, stayed fit and muscular. Sydney hardly saw him anymore, even though he was right next door. He started his shifts early in the morning before she was awake and the rest of the time he kept to himself. On a few occasions, in the early evenings after supper, she'd seen him through the window as she passed along the pathway in the garden, on her way out. He was sitting inside the enclosed porch with his parents, and each time she saw him he deked into the house to avoid seeing her. He seemed to be a different person since he'd come home—quiet and broody, a little melancholy. One day when Sydney and Deedee were coming home from the library together, arms stacked with books for themselves and Mum, Spencer hollered over to them grumpily saying, "All that reading is a waste of time."

Sydney had been so taken aback she didn't notice until after she was in the house he hadn't called her Frenchie. The name that used to annoy her so much was now a sign of affection and she felt wounded when he did not use it. Sensing she was losing a part of Spencer, she was surprised at how much more alone in the world she felt without him and so, she'd been delighted when he'd offered to take her to pick up the chair.

"All that Anna Karenina, Heathcliff, and Jane Austen you read and you still don't know your tributaries," Spencer said, teasing. She looked at him quizzically at the mention of the books she loved, surprised he knew them. "Yes," he said, surmising her thoughts—men look for answers too, Frenchie."

She let this sink in. "Have you found anyone yet, Spence?" She looked straight into his eyes when she asked him, even though she already knew the answer. "Have you started dating since you got home?"

River of Forgiveness

"Nah," Spencer said. "I need to find out who I am myself now, first." He breathed out. "The war. It changes you."

She remembered then, a letter he'd sent her, just after he'd enlisted. He was at Camp Borden at the time—the Canadian Forces base north of Toronto—receiving basic weapons training, so he hadn't had much time to write but he did send her a few letters the winter after he got there and one the following spring. He'd been so optimistic and uplifted, in a way she'd never heard him before. "I miss seeing your smiling face, Frenchie, waiting for me at school every morning but this is what I was born to do. I'm heading out tomorrow, assigned for duty on the front lines in Italy—all that hunting with Pops—and I am a natural with the 75 mm guns of these thirty-ton machines, it seems." A *joie de vivre* came across in his letters, for the first time, as if he'd found something he wanted or needed. Sydney hadn't understood it. Why a man would want to kill, to risk dying? It wasn't their country that was being invaded. Today, he seemed to be a changed man. He wouldn't speak of all he'd seen or done.

Sydney looked at his face closely; the lines, the creases around his eyes, a puffiness underneath, as though he weren't sleeping properly. "Were you scared?" she said.

"Not before I went," Spencer said.

"What about once you got there?"

"All the time. Night and day."

"How was it, you know, after D-Day? After you knew you were coming home?"

Kiidumae

"It was as if I left as a boy and came home as a man." Spencer took a long drag on his cigarette and didn't speak for a while. "I'm just not ready to settle yet," he said. "Got work down at the grain elevator. Got me my Ford and I've been meaning to tell you, I've bought land too—a little cabin back at Dorion. You'd love it there, Frenchie."

He told her about his camp. He said it was in canyon country, along the banks of the Wolf River and, in springtime, in the morning, it was so still you could hear the call of the loons. He said at night, the sky was littered with stars. He asked her if she remembered when they used to rise early to go smelt fishing before anyone else was up? Or Mudcat fishing at dusk?

"It's just like that out there, Frenchie," he said. "Peaceful and pure. Unadulterated by man or war."

For a moment, Sydney teared up. Something about the thought of those stars. When she and Spencer were children, they'd lie on the grass at night, looking for the North Star, the big and little dippers. She found herself wanting to be back under those stars. Something steady she could count on; never changing.

"It's gravity," Spencer said.

"Hmm?" Sydney said, wakened from her reverie.

"That's why the river flows back to the ocean." He told her when rain falls it either seeps into the ground or flows downhill, on its journey toward the seas. "Remember that from science class?" he asked.

"Not really," she said. "So, it's kind of like all that water is going back to where it came from. Back to where it belongs," Sydney mused, dreamily.

Spencer laughed. "Frenchie, you are hopeless," he teased. "Well, anyway, I love the river back at Dorion," he said. "It feels like where I belong. So maybe there is something to that romantic notion of yours."

"What do you do up there all day? By yourself, I mean."

"Winters I hunt, summers I fish."

"Doesn't it get boring?"

"Never," he said. "It's peaceful, it's challenging and it's physically demanding. It's not just sitting and looking at nature. You become a part of it, sort of in a symbiotic way and it gives you time to think, contemplate life."

"Is that where you plan to settle then?" she said. "All alone out there in the bush?"

"I've bought land in town here too," Spencer said proudly. "Over on Penfold Street. It's not much really—only just a small lot," he said, "but it's right next door to my brother, Alfred's place. Ma and Pop, they helped us each a bit with the purchase and I'm saving now, to build myself a house and a garden. I've always wanted my own garden."

It was the first time she'd seen him look so hopeful in a while.

"You'll make some girl very happy someday then," she said, "but it all sounds so, so, well...so final."

They didn't speak for several minutes. Their hands brushed lightly as they each shifted position, where they sat, side by side on Spencer's blanket, knees up, Sydney hugging hers, Spencer draped loosely across his. He lifted his right arm up and down in slow motion, each time he took a drag of his cigarette. He looked toward her.

"I'd always thought, before the war, well, I thought that"— his jaw tightened with emotion and quivered around his mouth as he fought to regain his composure—"...well, I thought maybe it'd be you and me," he said.

Sydney felt a sudden surge of emotion. Fear. That fear of losing him. Her eyes brimmed with unexpected tears.

"Ah, Spence," she said. She touched him gently on his forearm. It felt muscular and warm beneath his soft golden hairs under the morning sunlight. "You and me—we'll always be good friends, won't we? Can we—will we—stay friends?"

Spencer tugged at a dandelion poking up from the freshly groomed grass. He looked ahead, silent. A warm breeze caught a wisp of his fine blondish hair, blowing it up then back down again.

"I'm not going anywhere," he said softly, turning back to her. He smiled and squeezed her hand in his, like a bird's egg in need of protection. She saw that his eyes had glistened with tears. Sometimes she no longer understood him.

"Look at you, though," he said, his voice warbling. "You'll be a married woman in a week's time. Imagine that. My little Frenchie." He kissed the top of her forehead. "Well, we'd better go. Get you back in time for your shower, Princess."

"Yes," she said, beaming suddenly, choking back her own tears.

Chapter 13
Le téléphone

Sydney was appraising herself in front of the mirror—Maisie and Deedee on either side of her, adjusting her veil, crowned with a ring of white carnations and baby's breath. She applied foundation and dabbed at her nose with powder from her compact.

    It was at that moment the little green finch flew into the window on the back porch of the veranda and Mum became hysterical, thinking it to be an omen. Her nerves were in a jitter from the moment she'd risen in the morning, and she'd been pacing the house in her apron and slippers all day, busy with all the preparations, stabbing perpetually at her neck with iodine, her cheeks flushed from her rising blood pressure.

    Mum had come around though, got used to all the changes in a matter of months—the weddings, the arrival of her first grandchild, especially after the baby was born. Chuffy and Maisie's baby was a boy and Mum and Papa had both been delighted when they'd named it after him, another little Ambroise Jr. That seemed to raise Mum's spirits more than anything else ever could and so she got into the excitement of Sydney's nuptials, planning it with a zeal they had never seen in her before.

    A few weeks before the wedding, Papa had come home with a pup in his arms and a kitten in the tattered pocket of his overcoat. "Some company, for Deedee, now that she'll be the only one left home to roost," he said.

    Sydney surmised, though, it was also a ruse—to keep Deedee interested in something other than boys for as long as possible. The pup was a mutt of a thing, part Collie and parts of—who knew what else—so Mum and Deedee named him Haggis. The kitten was a smoky-grey color and Deedee called him Satchmo, "because Papa loves Louis Armstrong's music so much," she said.

    When the finch flew into the veranda, Haggis began to bark, as if he were thinking Mum was in some sort of danger, with her hollering the way she was. Satchmo jumped at the screen on the veranda door, hissing and meowing, trying to get at the little green finch and Ambroise Jr. joined in and started to wail, until Papa went in and rescued the little bird and then all the commotion died down.

River of Forgiveness

The telephone had been ringing cheerily all day and, thus, Sydney and her sisters, none of them, were surprised when the telephone rang again. She was still in front of the mirror, adjusting her veil when that last call came and she studied her reflection, so mesmerizing it took her own breath away. She was wearing only her white slip and brassiere, waiting until the very last minute before stepping into her dress, which had a long train behind but still, she thought she looked like a princess in a fairy tale with her crown on her head.

Maisie and Deedee were already in their bridesmaid dresses—too excited to wait. The deep fuchsia-colored satin, chosen by Sydney, was striking against the contrast of their fair complexions, as milky white as her veil.

The radio hummed softly and melodically in the background and Francis Craig and his Orchestra's *Near You*—the song Sydney had chosen for their first dance—began to play. She skipped across the room and turned up the volume. Her fiancé had wanted Pachelbel's Canon in D Major— "the best songs in the world, Loves, are songs without words," he'd said.

Sydney had won out, though—"the Canon is just too darned slow"—she'd said, and she and Maisie and Deedee sang along now, to *Near You*, in front of the mirror, holding up their hairbrushes as mock microphones:

There's just one place for me, near you
It's like heaven to be, near you
Times when we're apart

Kiidumae

I can face my heart
Say you'll never stray
More than just two lips away

If my hours could be spent near you
I'd be more than content near you
Make my life worthwhile
By telling me that I'll
Spend the rest of my days near you...

"Oh yeah, yeah, yeah," they crooned, and fell back on top of the bed, their laughter carrying down the hall to the kitchen.

Sydney heard the thump, thump each time the telephone rang, as Mum lumbered into the dining room to pick the receiver up off the wall. She was making all the food herself—no small feat with almost two hundred guests coming—and neighbors were calling, offering to stop by and help transport the meatloaves, scalloped potatoes, diced beet and celery salad, and fried chicken to the Ukrainian National Hall on Robertson Street. Mum made the matrimonial cake herself too—a three-tiered fruit cake that weighed heavy as Helka teetered out the door to take it to Sweet Dreams Catering & Bakery to be iced.

The doors of the beautiful new kitchen cabinets Papa had built for Mum on his off-hours banged constantly open and shut. The last-minute preparations seemed endless. Sydney and her sisters were happy to be sequestered off in their tiny bedroom, left to fuss with their dresses and apply their make-up. At the last minute, Sydney applied an extra puff of white powder from her compact onto her nose, trying to conceal the sprinkling of freckles that had cropped up in the spring sunshine. Elliott liked her skin best when it was "as pure white as a winter dove," he said, and she wanted to please him.

"There," she said. "Done. I'm ready."

Deedee ran out to get Papa's camera to snap a photograph of Sydney in her newly crowned veil when the telephone rang again. She picked up the receiver from the dining room wall as she flew past on her way back to the bedroom with the camera, snaffled from the spot where Papa kept it, safely guarded in his corner where he was still playing solitaire and smoking his pipe, waiting for the chaos to die down.

"Could I speak to Miss Sydney Archambault, please?" asked the voice of a young, polite-sounding gentleman.

"She's awfully busy right now sir—it's her wedding today, you see. Can I help you with something? I'm her sister." Deedee hesitated. "And her bridesmaid," she added proudly.

"No. No, thank you, but unfortunately, you cannot help me. It is imperative that I speak to Miss Sydney directly."

"Wait then, wait just a moment, please."

Mum emerged from her bedroom just then, wearing the new blue silk dress Aunt Bess had given her as a gift from the consignment store, to wear for the wedding. She reached for her apron to put on over her dress while she was still handling the food. She lifted a tray of sliced meat from the countertop, covered with waxed paper, and leaned forward to hand it to Spencer's brother Alfred, who was waiting at the door to transport it to the Legion Hall. Satchmo emerged from Deedee's bedroom, bouncing down the hall and up onto the front of Mum's dress, scratching at it with his claws as he clung onto it, running the silk into strands down her bosom, bounding for the tray of meat. Haggis started to bark, humping on Mum's leg, his nails digging into her nylon stockings, trying to get at Satchmo. Mum yelped and threw him down off her but the damage to the dress was already done.

"Oh that bloody cat," Mum screeched, the first time any of them had heard her curse. "Ambroise, what were you thinking, dragging that thing home? As if I don't have enough to worry about at a time like this. Deedee, put it back in your room. Right now," she snapped and stomped off to change into another dress.

Deedee pranced to the back bedroom with Satchmo, throwing him onto the bed, and called through the door to Sydney in a sing-songy voice, "Oh Sydney, it's *le téléphone*—for you-ou. There is a young man who absolutely insists he must speak directly with you."

Deedee smiled, knowingly. She'd only met Sydney's fiancé once and didn't recognize the voice but she thought it must be him. Who else would be calling so persistently? There was an air of mounting excitement in the house and she found herself humming with giddy anticipation.

Sydney's heart surged. Elliott. How she missed him. He had stayed firm in his conviction that they not see one another for a whole week before the wedding and it had been agonizing. He hadn't said anything about speaking on the telephone but he'd been out of town on business all week and this was the first time he had called. She rushed to the phone without thinking and Papa flushed when he saw her there in her underclothes.

"Oh," Sydney cried, and grabbed Papa's freshly pressed shirt, hanging on the back of one of the dining room chairs, waiting there for him to dress just before it was time to leave for St. Patrick's Cathedral. She wrapped it around herself.

Aunt Bess and Uncle Thierry had come from Winnipeg for the wedding. He was a guitarist in a band now and they were playing at the dance after the ceremony. He had joined Papa at the table for the wait. His face reddened too when he looked up and saw Sydney there and he sat with his head down tuning his instrument intently.

"Hello. Elliott? Elliott is that you?!" Sydney said excitedly.

"N-n-no, Miss Archambault. Is this Miss Sydney Archambault to who I am speaking?" His tone sounded grave.

"Yes, yes, this is Sydney. This is Miss Archambault."

"Uh, Miss Archambault, this is Felix here, "Felix Humboldt from Frank's Formal Wear?" He hesitated.

"Yes?" said Sydney. "Yes, we arranged for a rental from you a few months ago. Hopefully, there isn't a problem? Not now. Not today."

"Yes, yes," stuttered Felix. Um, well, that's just it, Miss Sydney, Miss Archambault, um, the tuxedo is still here, no problem, Miss Archambault."

Silence.

"Yes, well, the thing is, what it is, is that the tuxedo has not yet been picked up."

"Well, perhaps Mr. Caldwell has been delayed. Elliott Caldwell, my *fiancé*. He was to pick it up himself."

"Yes, yes, uh, that is exactly it, Miss Sydney," he said. "The tuxedo was to have been picked up before noon—"

"It is only just after two o'clock," Sydney snapped, her thoughts reeling. Waves of alarm tingled under her scalp. "Elliott is usually never late. He has never been late before," she cried out, registering the sound of fear in her own voice. A gurgling of saliva rose when she attempted to speak. She cleared her throat and then sucked in her breath to keep from hyperventilating, a habit since childhood, some inexplicable form of claustrophobia in moments such as this. She watched Papa's shirt rise and fall in front of her, on top of her breasts, the rapid beating of her own heart.

"Yes, yes, well, Miss Sydney, Miss Archambault, the tuxedo was to have been picked up before noon yesterday, you see, not today, the delay has been over twenty-four hours now."

Silence.

"Well, the thing is, Miss Archambault, I mean, if it was up to me, if these things were up to me, but they are not, the boss, Frank, my boss, the owner, he is very strict on policy and has told me I must release this tuxedo. I have another customer here, right now, standing in front of me, who is wanting it."

Silence.

"Do you understand Miss Sydney, can you hear me? I am so sorry, so very sorry."

Sydney slammed the phone down. Her heart pounded against her chest. She picked the receiver up again and dialed Elliott's number. It rang and rang. She rushed to the front hall closet, grabbed her tan spring coat, and threw it on over top of her slip and Papa's shirt. With trembling fingers, she slid into her white shoes with rubber soles, the ones she wore when she was working at the hospital laundry, and quickly tied the laces. She banged the front door shut behind her, and started to run. She ran past the Carrie-s-Corner Store and the Second Look Consignment Store, past a sea of blank, staring faces along the sidewalk, all the way past Reid's Countrywide Furniture where she and Elliott had ordered a chesterfield and a bed and a table and chairs that were to be delivered next week, on the first of June. She ran the whole way, straight to Elliott's apartment at Skyline Towers. He must be sick or hurt, something must be wrong. Tears streamed down her face, streaking her cheeks with chocolate lines of mascara, freshly applied at the hairdresser this morning. She pushed the buzzer of Elliott's apartment over, and over again.

Chapter 14
Skyline Towers – Through the Keyhole

Mum had moaned with relief when the green finch had flown away unharmed from the veranda that morning but she still fretted over what it meant—an omen of which she had forbidden anyone to speak. By that afternoon, the little finch was by now long forgotten, erased from everyone's memory, having been replaced by an air of excitement. A red-winged blackbird, speckled white under its wings, landed on the branch of a butternut tree beside Sydney, where she stood at the front door to Elliott's apartment building and she remembered the little finch, suddenly now.

Kiidumae

There was no reply when she buzzed Elliott's apartment. Finally, she rang the building superintendent who answered straight away. He let Sydney in and met her in front of Elliott's apartment door, carrying a large brass ring of master keys in his hand.

Sydney banged on the door and waited for a shadow of light to cover the peephole from inside but it didn't change, so she knew he wasn't there. A fear which she tried to squelch rose inside her. She asked the superintendent to open the suite, stepped inside, and broke into a smile when she saw that all of his things were still there.

"Oh," she cried with relief."

The superintendent looked down, as though he might cry. He told her she'd misunderstood. That Elliott Caldwell rented this room furnished. That these things were not his. He said the room was now exactly the way it was when Elliott moved into it—all of his own things—his clothes, toiletries, records. They were gone. He'd left a few days ago.

The super quietly slipped out, leaving her alone in the room—so quietly that she didn't even notice at first.

She looked around the room, more closely now, and saw that the cross, the one that had hung over the bed and always made her feel guilty, was no longer there. His record player was gone too. A bicycle bell chimed outside the window and, for a second, she thought she heard the music playing.

She walked through the apartment again, through the little nook of a kitchen with sunny yellow coffee mugs hanging from the cup hooks, through to the bathroom, and looked inside the medicine cabinet, now cleaned out of everything except for a little round stain where Elliott's toothbrush glass had sat. In the garbage can was a collection of ointment tubes and bottles, not yet emptied, items too small or used up to bother taking them with him and, in the middle was the bottle of cherry brandy, now emptied, the same little bottle they had drunk from before, to relax.

She walked back to the main room and found the broken plastic wand from the curtain rod on the floor under the window. It was the wand that Elliott had waved back and forth in time to the music while she watched him from his bed, his dark straight hair falling forward in his crazy and adorable impersonation of an impresario. That time it was not the Nocturne he was playing, it was Schubert's Standchen, as played by Franz Liszt—the solo piano version—and he'd played it over and over with a rising manic passion that enflamed her.

Nothing of Elliott's was left there. She turned to go, unbelievingly, when she saw the single sock tucked into the corner, under the bed, next to the brown metal bed frame. The last time she had been here, Elliott had been in such a rush of excitement to make love to her that he'd yanked it off and made a ball of it with his fist and threw it into the corner.

Sydney grabbed it out from under the bed and held the rough wool against her face and breathed in his familiar scent. She felt her insides weaken with a knowledge she was not yet ready to accept. She started to cry. She slunk slowly down to the floor and fell onto her knees. She heard a wailing sound and screaming—"no, no, no, no," like she sometimes heard when she was at work and the sound of primal agony came funneling down the corridor halls to the laundry at the hospital when someone died and their family had just come to visit and discovered their loved one was gone.

Her mind cleared, circling in on the cry of grief, and Sydney realized it was the sound of her own voice. A voice inside that seemed to be telling her everything does not always turn out all right. She felt the little happy hum of excitement she had woken up with that morning dissipate into a coagulated lump of pain in her throat and settle in, ready to stay. At the age of not yet twenty, life, life itself, had already broken her heart.

Chapter 15
To Our Family & Friends

It was Mum who had the wherewithal to write something, for there hadn't been much time—not enough time to call all of the guests individually and be certain they would be found at home, so she opted for a note. An announcement that she was too overcome with emotion to read once she came to stand in front of everyone at the church. It was the same spot where she'd stood during the rehearsal the week before, Sydney's conversion to Catholicism being now complete. They were not an overly religious family as far as a denomination was concerned but Mum hadn't enjoyed the conversion process. It was just that Elliott Caldwell had made that a stipulation. A ploy, Mum surmised later, to keep a hold on Sydney but, in the end, Mum had accepted it. What difference did religion make anyway, one Christian religion over another, when they all believed in the same things? And, Mum rather enjoyed the candles burning softly at the front of St. Patrick's Cathedral during the rehearsal, the breaking of the bread, the little sip of wine before they took communion. It somehow made the church feel that much more festive if festive was a word one might use to describe a church, befitting nonetheless for a church in which her firstborn child—her eldest daughter—was to be married.

On the wedding day, however, instead of watching Sydney marry, Mum got up in front of everyone with the note she had written. She stood, still wearing her blue and white floral cotton house dress she'd changed into after Satchmo had ruined her silk one, her hair disheveled from the day's events, bobby pins sticking out hither and thither, her hands trembling. She looked out into the pews at the sea of expectant faces, gathered there for a happy occasion, and a sudden feeling of foreboding came over her. It had all been just too much. She had thought she would be sobbing with joy by now, overcome by the beauty of her first-born daughter in her wedding dress and veil, now heaped in a pile in the corner of the bedroom, where Sydney was hiding out from the world. So Mum stayed standing at the front of the church, leaning forward to steady herself on the pew in the first row, and motioned for Helka to come up and read the note for her. Helka was, after all, to have been the maid of honor and somehow

Mum could not bear the pain of the thought of one of her other daughters, Maisie or Deedee, having to be the one to endure this humiliation for Sydney either. It had all been rather instinctive and reactive, Mum watching Helka sitting there, poised, her small hands in white gloves, elegantly clutching her handbag. Her spring dress, with a high white collar, her blonde hair freshly cut and styled that morning, a look of composure about her, of resolute calm in the face of tragedy. Thus, it was Helka that Mum beckoned to, waving her up with her tear-stained hanky, Mum clutching herself onto Helka's left arm as she read out, in a clear, succinct voice, the note that Mum had scrawled out in a hurry:

To Our Family & Friends,

We regret to have to inform you that, due to unforeseen circumstances, we have decided to cancel the forthcoming wedding of our daughter, Sydney Elizabeth Archambault to Elliott Edmond Caldwell, which was due to take place here, today, on Saturday, May the twenty-fourth, in the year of our Lord, nineteen hundred and forty-seven. We do thank you for your understanding during this difficult time and sincerely apologize for any inconvenience this may have caused.

Sincerely, Mr. & Mrs. Ambroise Archambault

After Helka finished reading the note there was a hush in the church and Helka added that Sydney had requested all gifts received be returned and this could be done tomorrow afternoon at the house between 2 and 5 o'clock.

Helka went back to her seat, not knowing what else to do, followed by Mum. A murmur of voices and uncomfortable glances circulated throughout the church, a supportive squeeze of Mum's shoulder by the person behind her. Papa sat slumped in the seat next to her, his head bowed in shame.

The priest quickly shifted roles. Turning to Mum and Papa, he said "My prayers are with you at this difficult time." He stood at the podium shuffling through his bible, and began reading from Proverbs:

"There are three things that are too amazing for me, four that I do not understand: the way of an eagle in the sky, the way of a snake on a rock, the way of a ship on the high seas, and the way of a man with a maiden…"

He read from Psalm 34:18:

The Lord is near to the brokenhearted and saves the crushed in spirit.

He concluded with, "May the Peace that passes all understanding be with you."

Later, wedding guests said it had been the sound of Mum's bawling, reverberating off the stained-glass ceiling of St. Patrick's Cathedral as they were ushered silently out the doors, that stayed with them long afterward.

    The next day Sydney dressed in the new clothes she'd bought for the train ride that was to have been to Niagara Falls—a light blue short-sleeved silk blouse with her pearls resting on her throat underneath, a matching dark blue plaid pleated wool skirt. She sat at the dining room table to deal with the steady stream of would-be wedding guests. She watched the parade of toasters and kettles and pewter serving trays make their way back out the door and down the path to the sidewalk, the same way in which they had come. It was hard for her to believe these items that once filled her with excitement at the anticipation of her new role and life as Mrs. Elliott Edmond Caldwell now felt to be meaningless trinkets. She did feel a twinge, here and there, as the pieces of her silverware, her crystal wine goblets, and her Lenox Rose china pattern—the ones she'd registered for at the Hudson's Bay Department Store—made their way past her in the arms of the original donors but then the memory would come back again and those twinges dissipated as quickly as they arrived.

    Some of the wedding guests, mercifully, did not come by at all, too humiliated for Sydney, or too humiliated for themselves, to benefit from her demise. By the end of the afternoon, she sat slouched at the dining room table in a weary state in front of the items that remained. Later, she would give these to Helka still unwrapped, not wanting the memory of their presence.

Kiidumae

When it was over, she broke down and cried; she'd held herself together all through the day, still in a state of shock, listening to the sympathies offered her, determined not to let them see the depth of her despair. She was humiliated beyond her own imagining.

Papa pulled a bottle of Cointreau from the bottom cupboard of the china cabinet and lifted two of Mum's little Baccarat cordial glasses, usually saved for special occasions—special happy occasions—from behind the glass on the upper shelf. He filled them and they sat at the table together in the darkened dining room and drank the liqueur. When Sydney was finished, they moved to the big cream-colored heirloom chair Aunt Bess had sent—the only wedding gift she would keep for the rest of her life—and she sat on Papa's knee, the way she used to when she was a child. She started to cry again, hard, laying her head on Papa's shoulder, where she fell asleep in his arms. Eventually, Papa rose and ushered her into the front room, gently laying her down on top of the sofa, still fully clothed. He kissed her cheek and tiptoed out, quietly closing the door behind him.

River of Forgiveness

Chapter 16
Deedee Answers the Door

Deedee was up earlier than usual, in the kitchen baking pies with freshly picked strawberries from the greenhouse in the garden and blueberries from the freezer. She hadn't been able to stand it anymore, morning after morning, night after night, listening to Sydney sobbing into her pillow, trying to stifle the sounds. Watching her back as it quivered up and down, the trembling spreading across the mattress and under the sheets—blowing her nose into the wrung-out hankies piling up on the floor beside her bed. Each day, a different color of embroidered initials—SEC—on the corner of the set of seven handkerchiefs Mum made her for her birthday in

April, to put in her hope chest—Sydney Elizabeth Caldwell.

The remainder of the household was out early, except for Papa who sat, as he always did on Saturday mornings—a first day's rest from his week working twelve-hour days at his carpentry job at the shipyards—playing games of solitaire, the cards laid out in front of him akin to a secret story being unfolded. The smoky smell of his pipe tobacco mingled with the scent of Deedee's pies baking in the oven. Mum had walked to the butcher shop to purchase pork chops for dinner. Sydney would normally be with Maisie at this time, where they both still worked at the hospital laundry, but she hadn't left her bed for the entire week.

"Why does she have to wallow in it so?" Deedee had asked Mum earlier that morning.

Mum sighed and shook her head in response. "I told her she should have married Spencer. He'll never have her now. No decent man likely will. Ah well, *Que Sera, Sera*," Mum said. "What will be, will be."

Mum had loaded and cocked Papa's Smith & Wesson shotgun and put it in the corner of the living room, next to the front door, ready to fire. "You let me know if that good-for-nothing Limey comes crawling back here," she shouted out to Deedee and Papa, slamming the front door behind her on her way out.

Deedee pulled the pies from the oven and jammed a fork into the middle of one. She sucked the blueberry juice from the fork and smiled. It was perfect. She scattered some more flour onto the surface of the counter and set two more rolls of dough out to make more pies—strawberry this time.

She heard a knock and looked over at Papa, still in the corner of the dining room playing cards, not to be disturbed. Deedee wiped the flour from her hands and went to the front door.

"It's a good thing your mother's not home," Papa said, as he glanced up at her. Flour was everywhere—in her hair, all over her clothes, the countertops, on the tile floor in the kitchen.

Haggis had come bounding out from his spot under Papa's chair at the sound of the knock on the door and skidded across the kitchen floor after Deedee, trotting through the dusty flour. Satchmo was close on his tail. Haggis barked as Deedee peered through the peephole at a tall middle-aged man standing there. She opened the door.

"Yes?" she said.

A man with the widest shoulders she'd ever seen stood before her wearing a no-nonsense officious expression on his face. He flashed a card with his identification. Reginald Hunt. Private Detective.

"I'm looking for an Elliott Edmond Caldwell," he said. "Do you know where he is?"

"No," Deedee said. "And he'd better not show up around here either. He jilted my sister a week ago and my mother has a shotgun loaded and said she's going to use it too if he ever steps foot on our front porch again."

Reginald Hunt snickered as he handed her a card with his phone number and address, with a photograph of himself on the corner of the card, looking much younger than he did now.

"Call me if you see him. His wife's looking for him."

Deedee flinched. She slipped the card into the pocket of her white apron. "All right, I will."

Sydney had rushed to the bedroom door in her nightgown and opened it a crack to listen when she'd heard the knock on the door. She thought it might be Elliott. That he might have come back for her. She thought she had already heard the worst though, that it couldn't possibly get any worse until she eavesdropped on what Reginald Hunt had to say.

The worst of it was not that Elliott Caldwell had jilted her, practically at the altar, as it were, or even finding out that he was already married. The worst of it was she would never see him again—that the sudden, spontaneous, passion he had ignited in her, that she was not yet done with, her body still yearning to have him there, would never again be. To never see his face, to never again know his kiss on her face, just one more time, to not be able to see it through, or talk to him—that was the worst of it.

"Is there a Miss Sydney Archambault at this address then?" Reginald Hunt asked Deedee.

Sydney stepped forward, still in her nightgown, expectant.

"The superintendent from Skyline Towers asked me to give this to you if Mr. Caldwell wasn't here," he said. He handed her a small box addressed to a Robert Holley. "It's a few of his things, sent over from the camp when they closed it down."

Sydney didn't speak for a few minutes. She stood, frozen, her mouth agape. "Camp? What camp?" she said.

"...Camp R." Reginald Hunt said. "Didn't you know?"

Sydney felt the color fade from her face and her ears started to ring. "No. No," she whispered. She began to quiver.

"Well, I guess three men can keep a secret if two of them are dead." He laughed, amused with himself over his own joke.

"What...what type of a camp is it?" she said. "Do you mean a hunting camp? I don't understand." Even as she asked the question, she wasn't sure she wanted to know.

"The internment camp. Over on Lake Superior. It was a prisoner of war camp. Mostly a bunch of Brits who were shipped over by Churchill at the start of the war. About sixty or so miles northeast of here."

Sydney had no idea about what Reginald Hunt was talking. Afterward, she went back to bed, doubled over and holding her stomach. The pain was making her physically sick. She lay in the fetal position, rocking herself. It seemed the tears would never stop coming. There seemed no way out of this abyss she had stepped into. She needed to see him again. She needed an explanation. She needed to know why and what was happening. She didn't care what he had done. She just had to see him.

Chapter 17
The Black Fox Inn

Sydney approached the reservation desk in the main dining room of the Black Fox Inn and asked for him by name. Her white-gloved hands clutched her evening bag more tightly than was necessary. She was trembling again. The attention she had paid to her appearance was obvious. Her dark hair was permed and curled into soft waves, not a strand was out of place. The dress she had chosen was his favorite, chocolate brown, accentuating her figure, slightly low at the bodice.

"Your body is a perfect Stradivarius," he'd told her once, as he'd caressed her skin, running his middle finger down the side of her hip, like the bow of a violin.

On her throat was the string of pearls Mum and Papa had given her as a gift on her high school graduation. At the last moment, she placed the fourteen-karat gold frog charm over top of her pearls for good luck, a gift from Spencer on that same graduation. It was engraved on the back, with *Frenchie*. He'd sent it to her, all the way over from France, during the war.

Sydney didn't look around for Elliott, she didn't want to appear too anxious or obvious, although she knew he must be there. Spencer had arranged this meeting. She'd pleaded with him to help her—she could no longer stand it—and Spencer fulfilled her wish somehow—how, she didn't want to know.

When she was with Spencer it was as if the sun were always shining, she could be herself, and she could talk to him so easily but there was still none of that magical feeling as there was when she was with Elliott and her heart pounded at the thought of seeing him.

Sydney looked across the restaurant toward the window, as the *maître'd* said, "right this way, miss."

She'd only half expected he would actually be there. He sat at a table in the far corner, hands clasped in front of him, looking rather wrung out. Elliott was not looking about the room, in anticipation, as one might expect, but he seemed as though he might be waiting for someone; he kept checking his watch. She wondered whether he had come, hoping to see her there as she hoped to see him.

Sydney had imagined this moment over and over again, all week. There was a landscape painting on the wall in Elliott's apartment she'd admired. She pictured meeting him in that painting, on the path it showed; she imagined their joy, their shyness in bumping against one another; but she knew they were not to be.

Joy flooded her heart, though, at the sight of him, she rushed toward his table, still shaking. She wasn't certain what Spencer had said or done to get him here but was grateful for it. As she approached the table, Elliott did not look up and did not smile, or seem happy to see her even. He looked surprised and a bit angry. Composing his expression, he went to say something as he stood to greet her but didn't finish his sentence. He did not embrace her, as he normally did when she met him at his apartment.

"Sydney," he said, in such a way it seemed he was not certain what to do or say next, more of a question. Distanced. "Sit down," he said, with an uncustomary formality, motioning to the seat beside him.

Sitting next to him was the most natural thing in the world, it felt to be her place; when she was there, she was where she wanted to be and never wanted to leave.

Elliott did not look into her eyes or comment on her appearance or even seem to notice her physically, at all. For the first time since they'd met each other, his eyes seemed vacant.

"Shall we order a drink?" he asked.

Elliott ordered a double shot of Smirnoff's, as he always did when he was out, and Sydney ordered a Grasshopper Cocktail. They sipped in silence for a few moments. Elliott looked down at the table.

"I…I'm sorry if I hurt you," he said finally. He looked as though he might cry. "I don't want to hurt anyone. I don't want to hurt my family, my in-laws. I want people to like me. I care what people think of me. That's changing as I get older, not as much as before, but I'm a Catholic, maybe if I wasn't a Catholic…"

Elliott was rambling. His face, under the glare of the too-bright chandelier, looked ravaged and defeated. Against her own will, her heart went out to him and, for a moment, incomprehensibly, she was left feeling as though she was the one who'd hurt him.

"Well, you did hurt me," Sydney replied, looking off to the side. She was resolute, holding her emotions in check. She wondered how she figured into his estimation of not hurting anyone. What about her?

"It wouldn't be the same, Sydney. I wouldn't be the same person I am now if I did what I would have to do to be with you. Can't you understand? Can't you just go back to the way it was? The way things were? Before you knew me? We'll probably laugh about this when we get older," he said and looked as though he might cry.

Sydney felt any glimmer of hope fade. A feeling of sadness began to settle into her throat and make its way up toward her eyes, down into her heart. She bit her lower lip. She wasn't going to cry. She looked into his eyes.

"No," she said softly. "It's not the same." Her voice dropped to a whisper. "Nothing will ever be the same again."

Elliott looked put upon. "Well, snap out of it," he said and quickly rose to his feet. He snatched an envelope from his breast pocket and thrust it at her, "*For Sydney*" scrawled across it and underlined. He threw a few dollars down onto the table. He no longer looked as if he might cry. He embraced Sydney, a friendship hug, taking care not to touch his body against hers and, with that, he was gone.

Sickened, a swell of nausea rose to her throat. She wanted to believe him, even as she knew she would never see or hear from him again.

Sydney had always evaded people who wore a weight of heavy tragedy about them and she certainly never thought of herself as one of them; but she began to see herself that way now and she thought others were recoiling from her as she staggered through the Black Fox Inn, out the front door, to the parking lot, where Spencer sat in his red Ford pickup truck waiting for her. He wrapped his arms around her as she climbed in and she cried hard, soaking the shoulder of his wool coat.

"Aw," he said. "This was a bad one." Spencer ran his thick finger across the bridge of Sydney's nose, gently stroking the splattering of freckles that had cropped up there—light little beauty marks he'd always loved, sprinkled over her small nose that made her seem sweet and innocent as a child.

"Elliott thought he was meeting me, Sydney," Spencer said. "I told him I had a big order of door viewers, a whole apartment building's worth. I had to think of something—I had to tell him something to get him here. I'm so sorry."

"It's all right," she said. "I needed to come. I needed to see him." She wiped her nose. "I needed to know." She started to weep again. Spencer rubbed her shoulder gently, kneading it with his thumb to calm her and held out tissue after tissue until she'd cried herself out.

Chapter 18
On the Rebound

Exactly six months later, on the twenty-ninth of November, Sydney married Spencer. It was the only thing for her to do. She felt reassured by him, his being there, the companionship she'd come to rely on, keeping a balance, a rhythm, a regulating that allowed her, enabled her, to go on.

"Do you really think I should?" she'd asked Deedee after he'd proposed to her. "Am I being fair to him?"

"Go on and marry him, Sydney," she'd said. "Be a good wife to him. He's been in love with you since the eighth grade and has enough love for the both of you, in any case."

She'd asked Spencer, too, if he was sure. If he could live with it.

"I'm more worldly now," he'd said, looking down into his lap. "In France and Italy—I...I've been with others too." He flushed red. "But they only made me think of you..." He looked up at her, straight into her eyes. "Frenchie, with you I'll be as settled as I always wanted to be."

So, in the end, she'd relented. They both loved children and there was a solace and optimism—pragmatism even—at the thought of the family they could build together.

They had a small wedding in Spencer's mother's living room with only family and close friends in attendance—Helka as her maid of honor, Spencer's brother Alfred the best man. Sydney could no longer bear to step into a church, any church, an aversion that would stay with her for the rest of her life and, thus, the Wesley Street United Church, despite Mum's protestations, was completely out of the question.

"*Que Sera Sera*," Mum said to her afterward at the reception, beaming but choosing not to say it, not to lord it over her that she'd been right about Spencer from the very beginning. Later, that song, and other music she had listened to with Elliott, would always make her cry. It implied some lightness or simplicity about love and life, of which, for Sydney, there was no longer either.

On the way out to Spencer's camp at Dorion for their honeymoon, bumping along the icy roads in the pickup, at times Sydney felt as though she might slink to the floor of the truck and never be able to get back up again, never be able to fully bounce back.

Sometimes, later, on their regular trips out to the cabin, Sydney wondered who she really was—living out this life through her actions and her motions and yet, inside, feeling as though she belonged to someone else, somewhere else.

It was Spencer who had found out for her about the internment camp, somehow, through his connections in the army. He'd told her how, for eighteen months during the war, the Canadian military held 1,150 prisoners in the camp in Red Rock.

"It seems that 'Camp R' interned friend and foe alike," Spencer said. "Churchill shipped over Nazis, anti-Nazis, Jews, soldiers, merchant seamen, you name it. Refugees who Britain feared might be part of Hitler's rumored "fifth column"—alien enemies residing in the Commonwealth. Our Mr. Caldwell, it seems, was in that latter category—and a Catholic, so nothing to fear, I'm happy to say."

Sydney could have cared less about any of it. Anything to do with the war. She only cared about hearing more news about her Elliott. She read the letter he'd given her at the restaurant over and over again until eventually she had memorized it completely then she thought about it all the time, mulling over his words in her head constantly, trying hard to comprehend. Trying to understand how she could not have known, not have sensed it.

My Dearest Sydney,

I have given this letter to Spencer to pass on to you on my behalf because I know how much he cares for you and I want him to be present, to be there to console you where I cannot after you have finished reading what I have to say. Please forgive my cowardice in not facing you myself.

Before I begin what it is I have to tell you, I would like to start by saying, shortly before our wedding was to have been, you asked me if I loved you, and I want you to know that I do. That much I know in my own heart and the reason I could not say it to you is that I had begun to feel as though I was deceiving you and this, from the very beginning, was never my intent.

I sincerely regret having to write this letter to you and am ashamed beyond belief at what I have done. I hope you can find it somewhere within yourself to forgive me, or I hope, at least, that you might try to understand.

So let us begin with the truth. Firstly, I come from Leeds, in London, England, that is where I was born. That much of what I've told you is true. My name is Robert Edmond Holley and, before you think I am someone who I am not, let me say that the only reason I began to use an alias was to protect you and, in truth, to conceal who I was so I could start anew.

In the spring of 1940, before I was arrested as an enemy alien by the British Government and sent to the prison camp in Red Rock, I was a law student at Cambridge University in London. At that time, I had been married for just over a year to Elsa Stotter. We'd met in our first year of university and shared a love of chess and so, we both had joined the campus chess club. Elsa graduated a year before I did, and began teaching reception, supporting me financially while I finished law school. Our intent, shortly before we were parted, was to begin a family as soon as I graduated, something we both cherished.

Elsa's family had emigrated to England as refugees but both of us had been cleared through the tribunal at the start of the war. Once Churchill had decided to incarcerate those of us on that list, there was no attempt made to keep married couples together and, thus, Elsa and I were separated and sent to different camps.

When Red Rock was being closed down and I was to be transferred to the internment camp at Petawawa, I escaped. Since then, I hadn't had word from Elsa throughout the war, nor did I try to contact her, since I no longer knew where she was and did not want to put her in any danger. I thought about going back, after the internment camps closed, at the end of the war. I thought of returning home, to England.

At this juncture, I feel I need to tell you that, after a year and a half at Red Rock and, left as a virtual fugitive, I was no longer the man I once had been. The lightness and optimism with which I once viewed the world was replaced by something else—a form of glibness had set in, survival, perhaps? You'll never know, Sydney. I hope you'll never know. While I was a prisoner in the camp, I thought only of Elsa and I awaited my release so we could be reunited. Afterward, though, I'm ashamed to admit, before you, I bedded women I never loved because I am a man, Sydney, and a man has his needs. Animalistic longings that no man—no man— can live without. I cannot say I am proud of that baseness, that beastly side of humanity and might never have known it existed within me if it weren't for the war. It has changed me. I was no longer the same man and I didn't know if I could ever face Elsa again, after what I had done. It seemed prudent to start life anew.

That was at the time I met you. I'd only just begun my business, an opportunity, I thought, because of the peddlers and hobos that had emerged during and after the war years. I felt optimism for life again, with you, finding love again. It seemed to me to be more natural to go forward, rather than backward. With you, it was different. It was not like the other women I'd had since Elsa, women who were there only to see me through that time of loneliness. I loved you. And *though I will never now admit it to her, I've loved you more than her.*

That is the time when Betty Blackwell came to find me. She'd been tracking me, with the British and Canadian Governments. Elsa was looking for me. You see, it seemed she'd been with child at the time we separated and of course I had no way to know. And so, she'd borne me a son, Sydney, and not just one, but two. Twins. Twin boys.

Still, I didn't want to know. I wanted to start my life over again. I loved you and I wanted to be with only you. I've never known such love before. With Elsa, it was different. I was young and we liked the same things. There was a comfort there and she was good—a good Catholic girl.

Betty Blackwell came back, to see me at my apartment, and she brought photographs. Pictures of Elsa and my sons. She'd named them Benjamin and Alexander. Sydney, when I saw that photograph it was as though I were looking back at my own soul. It made me feel young again. It made me feel like maybe I could be that hopeful, optimistic man I once was, again. And so, I had to make a choice. I had already made my commitment to Elsa; we were already married and there is more, Sydney. She'd been injured by a piece of shrapnel in a raid during the war and it has affected her mobility. This is what I've been told. I haven't seen her yet but she is alone—injured and alone with our two sons.

I tried to tell you all of this when we were together but then I'd see you again and I'd delay again. For just one more time I kept telling myself. But once Elsa had found me, I knew I could not, in all good conscience, go on deceiving you.

The war, Sydney—all that you see. It makes it seem like life, that other life, your life before the war, was so very long ago; another lifetime ago—and, well, it is easy to forget and harder to remember that it ever existed.

But I kept thinking if I chose to ignore it, and she kept coming back, more insistently, the longer you and I were together, the worse it would be.

I am so truly sorry, from the bottom of my heart, Sydney, that I have deceived you. I know that I will carry your heart in mine for as long as I live and that is to be my penance for what I have done.

As for you Sydney, I reason to myself, I justify it to myself, by saying you are young. You are young and so beautiful; a beauty that will catch the hearts of many. You can start again. You can forget I ever existed—thrust me from your mind and heart forever, and start anew. This is what you must do.

In closing, there is nothing else for me to say other than to beg your forgiveness. This you must do, not for me, Sydney, it is something you must do for yourself.

It is doubtful we shall ever meet again but your heart will always be with mine. That, I do know. Forgive me too, for ending this letter with e.e., for I know no other way to say goodbye.

With all my love, always and forever,
Elliott

River of Forgiveness

somewhere i have never travelled,gladly beyond

e. e. cummings

somewhere i have never travelled,gladly beyond
any experience,your eyes have their silence:
in your most frail gesture are things which enclose me,
or which i cannot touch because they are too near

your slightest look easily will unclose me
though i have closed myself as fingers,
you open always petal by petal myself as Spring opens
(touching skilfully,mysteriously)her first rose

or if your wish be to close me,i and
my life will shut very beautifully,suddenly,
as when the heart of this flower imagines
the snow carefully everywhere descending;

nothing which we are to perceive in this world equals
the power of your intense fragility:whose texture
compels me with the colour of its countries,
rendering death and forever with each breathing

(i do not know what it is about you that closes
and opens;only something in me understands
the voice of your eyes is deeper than all roses)
nobody,not even the rain,has such small hands

Kiidumae

In the small box of items that Reginald Hunt had given her were Elliott's personal belongings from Red Rock—his immigration papers, medical records, a small capsule with prescription medication inside, a few of his books, a small framed photograph. It was a picture of a slim blonde girl, smiling with her head tossed back teasingly, her right leg bent at the knee in a mock pose, standing in front of a bank of lockers in the hallway of a school. Her hair was tied loosely up at the back and she looked radiantly happy. Elsa. Sydney surmised it must be her.

The morning after their wedding day Sydney sat, shivering, on an old rough blanket on the spring bed in Spencer's cabin, waiting for the eggs to thaw. She'd set them on the windowsill along with the coffee cream when they'd arrived the night before, and both were frozen solid. She watched the waves through the window, from the late fall winds that blew across Wolf River at Dorion—washing away the minutes, the hours, the days of her life, until one day—the day she waited for—she could finally just lie down and the pull of gravity would wash her away again.

With Spencer there was no music, no impresario, there were no songs without words, there were no words, there was only silence, save for the lonely creaking of the old metal bed and the occasional bump, bump of the loosening headboard as it banged against the wall. Wedging his knee firmly between hers, opening her up to him, her first inclination had been to resist—it was as though he were entering into Elliott's turf, trespassing on the part of her that was already taken. She relented because she knew she must; this, the beginning of what their love-making was to entail—Spencer, perspiring heavily through his sandy hair, quietness except for the pleading urgency of his breath, his whimper of gratitude as he came too quickly, making him seem weak—in his desire for her he'd justify his speedy crumbling to her, making Sydney feel awful that such things mattered at all to her. So, blessedly, it was over quickly and she'd pushed him off and away from her, telling him she could no longer breathe. She'd had to try hard to not let him know that she was crying.

At first, Sydney got through it by pretending he was Elliott. Then, after a while, there remained only her and Spencer in the hush and the stillness of their bedroom, a curtain of silence that prevailed for some time as Sydney limply held onto Spencer's back, tears streaming down her cheeks, waiting until he expired himself at last. Afterward, she'd feel sorry for him, hating herself for it and she'd curl her body into the back of his. She'd lay her arm over his waist and stroke and caress him gently, filled with self-loathing until they both fell asleep.

When back to the little house Spencer and his friends had built for them on Penfold Street, Spencer retreated to the basement with his beer and carpentry. Canisters of crafted wooden spoons in various stages of completion sat everywhere. Fishing flies, hardened with Sydney's red nail polish, collected in piles in little jars along the edge of his tool-shop window, next to a string of war medals from France and Italy—medals of bravery he'd never told her he'd earned or what they were for—that was Spencer.

He didn't want Sydney to work and so she immediately quit her job at the laundry. It was a relief not to have to go back there. Not to have to face everyone she had worked with, trying to avert their sometimes sorrowful, sometimes sympathetic, sometimes disdaining glances when she ran into them on the street.

Sydney stayed upstairs, eating candy, reading books from the library and, later, after Spencer had bought her a television set, watching movies, romance stories that invariably made her sad, made her cry. On his way to bed, Spencer stopped by the couch where she lay and covered her with a blanket where she had fallen asleep.

Surprisingly, it was only Spencer who seemed to understand what it meant to live with her insidious and quiet agony. Sometimes his tenderness and endearing rituals of care filled her with a tearful sense of gratitude. He had, after all, rescued her where many a man would not. At other times it filled her with a resentment that made her want to push him and his happy chatter away; the thought she would have to wait until there were enough new memories to cover over those memories with Elliott before she could begin living again filled her with fear.

Chapter 19
Following the Frogs

That first Christmas, less than a month after their honeymoon, Sydney ambled through the departments at the Hudson's Bay store, trying to find inspiration for a gift for Spencer. Everything seemed to make her think of Elliott. She found herself wondering if she knew, even after all these years, who Spencer really was. In their marriage, other than when they were having sex, she always felt good when she was with him. She felt true to herself, no putting on airs, and he was kind and respectful. In the end, though, the only items she had chosen for Christmas gifts she knew he would like were things he would use at his work in his newly promoted foreman's job at the

Grain Elevator; plaid flannel shirts, a metal lunch bucket that swung open on hinges, painted in a gunmetal blue enamel with a matching soup thermos, nuts you needed to crack open yourself and a hunting magazine for his stocking.

Sydney bypassed the rows of small kitchen appliances—neatly stacked shelves of toasters and coffee percolators and can openers. Benign items that one would never believe could evoke such sadness. It was hard for her to believe it had been less than a year ago, not even seven months.

Everyone said she had married Spencer too quickly afterward. This was said with a tone of "what kind of a person are you? Who can switch their emotions from one man to another at the drop of a hat?" A girl on the rebound, as though it were Spencer who was the victim here, not her and, perhaps on some level, they were right but she needed him. She needed Spencer's continued quiet reassurance that everything would be all right.

Sifting through the clothing racks at the Hudson's Bay, Sydney distinguished between the silk shirts she would have bought for Elliott and the flannel plaid ones she had chosen for Spencer and cologne—Elliott's light scent of Christian Dior he always wore. The whiff of it she'd inhaled into her nostrils when she passed by the cosmetics counter stung her eyes at the memory.

"Men's cologne, ugh." Spencer would scoff, "is for sissies. It's unmanly."

So she'd slipped an Old Spice Christmas gift set for Spencer into her shopping basket instead, products he always used. Practical, yes. That was Spencer. That was who he was.

It smelled to be a personal assault compared to Elliott's musky, male scent. Spencer used the same brand of soap for shaving, whisking it about in a mug with his shaving brush, cleansing his whiskers off down to soft skin, morning and night. She missed the masculine touch of Elliott's light whiskers bristling against her cheek when he kissed her, the roughness of his skin underneath.

It was only the hunting magazine for Spencer that caught Sydney's eye in the book department. The fishing magazines were seasonal and there were none out yet. She passed all of the magazines Elliott used to have piled up by his bedside, magazines accumulated to pass the time in motel rooms as he traveled from town to town, installing peepholes in nervous old ladies doors—music magazines, *Time, Life,* and *The Economist*; and books—he'd been reading Steinbeck's *The Wayward Bus* just before he left, and the sight of it still on the best sellers wall caused a twinge as Sydney stood looking at it.

She caved, remembering her first Christmas with Elliott when she spotted e.e. cummings on the bookshelves. Spencer had only one book—a large reference book from the National Rifle Association in the United States. Sydney thought of a joke she'd heard. 'I just don't know what to get my husband for Christmas,' exclaims the wife. 'How about a book?' replies her friend, sitting on the bus next to her. After a long pause the wife says, 'no, I don't think so. He already has a book.'

Kiidumae

"Reading is a complete waste of time," Spencer still always said, as though the things he occupied his time with were of much greater importance. *Just exactly what is it Spencer considers to be a good use of his time* she wondered? He saw some things as frivolous and extravagant now, compared to what he'd seen in the war; but he would never explain these things to her and so it was impossible for her to understand him.

In front of the book department, there were still those same few tables piled high with the games there had been the previous Christmas when she'd bought Elliott the chess set. The only games Spencer played were card games—Poker with his brother Alfred and 'the boys' on Friday nights while she read her library books. When she saw the chess set again it all came back to her. She could hear Chopin's music and see Elliott sitting next to her on the bed, naked, a sheet wrapped around his groin, the dark hairs of his long legs stretched out in front of him as he leaned back on the pillows, she, next to him on her side of the bed, naked also, bathed in soft light. Elliott the King and she the Queen—his Cheshire Queen.

When Sydney finally looked up from the games piled on the table, she was weeping. She rushed to the washroom and closed herself into one of the stalls with a slam of the door. She sobbed and moaned as she fell to her knees. She heard a hush of silence as everyone else in the ladies room ceased speaking—the mother in the stall next to her, giving instructions to her small daughter on flushing the toilet, went still. Sydney didn't care. She couldn't stop herself. The emotions she had been blocking out since she had married Spencer wailed out of her, echoing with what seemed to be deafening, final clarity, off the tile walls in the Hudson's Bay ladies room.

On their first Christmas morning together, Spencer gave Sydney a sewing machine. "It will give you something to do. Something constructive," he'd said, as she opened it.

He'd given her a frog, the first of what would become the beginning of a collection given every birthday and every Christmas—a collection she would eventually grow tired of but would never have the heart to tell him—this first one, speckled black on its back, ceramic, and open in the middle, ready to sit on the edge of her kitchen counter next to the sink, its' hungry mouth accepting inside a metal pot scrubber that was replaced each year in her stocking with one of a different color. This year, the first one was a sunny, happy yellow—defying a happiness Sydney reluctantly felt after she'd opened it.

In her stocking was a book of crossword puzzles.

Spencer's practicality had made her stop and ponder as she sat next to the Christmas tree—she wondered what anything in life could mean when something that had seemed so big in her life, so great, had turned out to be nothing at all. How was she to find meaning in these small things, these trinkets? She'd thought then *maybe nothing in life ever does really happen, nothing but a realization here, a mood there, a picture glimpsed of what was yet to come.*

Chapter 20
Dr. Montemueller

Sydney chewed her gum constantly as she flipped through *Cosmopolitan* magazine and swung her leg rapidly, the rubber from her white hospital shoes she still wore kicking at the leg of the coffee table as her foot went back and forth.

The receptionist pulled the next medical record from the tray. "Mrs. Frye?" She looked over her spectacles in Sydney's direction.

Sydney rose from her chair and approached the reception desk.

"I'm Mrs. Frye," she said, awkwardly. She still wasn't used to her changed name, to Spencer's name. She'd conditioned herself, joyously, for all those months, to the day she would be called "Mrs. Caldwell."

She thought she saw the receptionist sneer at her, her upper lip curled in disgust. Must have heard the whole story from the doctor, Sydney surmised. The receptionist rose from her chair.

"Right this way," she said, leading Sydney to a small room with an examining table. It was the same room she had waited in a few weeks ago when she'd first come in to see Dr. Montemueller about her flu symptoms. She'd steadily been losing her appetite and felt nauseated and feverish. Her muscles ached. She felt tired all the time. Spencer constantly chided her about how she picked at the food on her plate and how thin she was getting.

Dr. Montemueller entered the room. He greeted her and asked her how she was feeling. He cleared his throat as if he had something stuck in it.

She told him she wasn't feeling much better than last time, actually, no better at all.

"I'm not surprised," Dr. Montemueller said, clearing his throat again. "Sydney, I've known you since before you were born, when your mother came to see me, expecting you." He stopped and looked down. He seemed to be stalling the delivery of whatever it was he had to say. "This truly pains me to have to be the one to tell you." She held her breath. "That rash you have. Have you heard of syphilis?"

Sydney reeled around in her chair to face Dr. Montemueller. She opened her mouth three times before she finally spoke.

"Well, yes, of course. Mum told me when I came of age. And I've read a bit about it." She didn't ask why. She couldn't bring herself to—she already knew. "What does this mean then?" Sydney asked, finally. "I don't remember. Is there a cure? Will it go away?"

"We can treat it with anti-biotics and this cream, for your rash," he said, holding out a prescription and a tub of ointment for her. "It will subside in time. It should heal in about four to six weeks." He hesitated. "But there's something else you need to know."

Sydney waited.

"It's possible, not one hundred percent now, mind you."

She waited.

"It's possible that this may affect your ability to carry a child." Dr. Montemueller blurted the words out quickly, to get it over with.

Blood flushed hot up into Sydney's face. She hadn't wanted to gasp but she knew she must have when she looked into Dr. Montemueller's face and saw him wince. She felt shocked. This couldn't be real.

"I'm sorry Sydney."

She slid down off the examining table, her head hung low.

"Oh, and Sydney." Dr. Montemueller couldn't look at her then. She had started to cry.

"You must...you...you should abstain from intercourse for several weeks. Until the symptoms have disappeared." Dr. Montemueller looked weary. "You don't want this to pass on to Spencer."

Sydney left Dr. Montemueller's office and felt woozy as she stepped into the elevator. She had planned to take the bus home but she didn't want to wait. It was drizzling outside. Sydney walked all the way home—the mist on her face fresh and cleansing. Tears streamed hot down her cheeks and mixed with the cool raindrops. She thought of the day after she and Elliott had made love and he'd walked her home in the rain. How their bodies had jostled comfortably into each other, as though they were one. How the feel of his warm mouth had mixed with the warm rain. She looked up ahead and for a moment thought she saw him there with his umbrella walking toward her. She started to walk faster then began to run toward him but when she got to the spot where she'd thought she'd seen him, there was no one there. She walked around in a circle and back again, to where she had stood. She was sure she had seen him. She was certain he'd been there. She wanted the rain to cleanse her. She wanted it to pour down over her and run down through her hair and under her coat and blouse and bathe her body in fresh cool water. To wash away all the filth Elliott Caldwell had left all over her genitals and inside her body. To wash away all he had taken from her, all of what he had robbed her.

On her way out the door, Dr. Montemueller had stopped her and put a hand on her shoulder. He'd said, with the ways of the world, you are left to discover them for yourself. You approach the world with a trusting heart, he'd said, a childlike innocence that doesn't go away, left to your own instincts until something happens that alters and changes who you are. He'd stumbled over his words, trying, in his own way to vindicate her of her foolish actions.

Sydney's pace accelerated and soon she was running again. Wavelets of rain, as it grew heavier, matted her hair and streamed down her face. She rushed into the front door of their little house at 189 Penfold Street and kicked off her hospital shoes, caked in mud. She threw her coat into a heap on the floor and stormed into the kitchen.

"Spencer," Sydney screamed. He wasn't there.

She made her way into the living room. There Spencer sat in one of the turquoise revolving side chairs where they spent their Sunday mornings together, reading the newspaper and drinking coffee. He put the paper down and looked up at her.

"Sydney? Oh, my darling little Frenchie, what is it?"

She threw herself on her knees in front of Spencer's chair, her head in his lap, and wailed. Spencer stroked her wet hair. He wanted to rise and get a towel but didn't want to move her. She cried hard into his chest, with her fists clenched onto the back of his shirt. He knew not to ask what it was. He felt a beat skip in his chest and a hollow feeling. Instinctively, he knew whatever had gone before, the worst of it was heaped right here and now on his lap. Silently, he cursed Elliott Caldwell.

Chapter 21
The Other Side of Spencer

It was the ninth of April, Sydney's birthday, and Spencer was taking her to dinner at the restaurant in the Cascades Motel at Kakabeka Falls. Sydney was in a bit of a sullen mood and had to feign excitement. The Cascades was where she'd last gone with Elliott on New Year's Day. It seemed everywhere they'd ever gone together was marked, akin to an animal leaving its scent; each spot and the memory of it now permanently placed and its richness could not be replaced.

    Spencer noticed her mood and tried to make light of it, to pull her out of that secret place he knew the source of but could never enter.

"Ah, c'mon Frenchie," he teased, tickling her a little. "Cheer up, you're not that old yet," he said and winked.

Sydney felt her face flush and, unexpectedly, wanted to turn and push him away. It was her time of the month and she always seemed to find some reason to get upset. It was a mixture of gratitude at having Spencer there to love her so dearly, so unconditionally, and contentment blended with sadness at never really seeming to be present enough to enjoy or appreciate it. It was as though she were being disloyal to herself—that she wasn't being true to herself being in love with someone else and it was the pain, too. Spencer's pain in his knowledge of that.

"Here, I've bought you a present."

He pulled a card and a small box from his jacket pocket. He'd dressed in his good grey suit, the one he'd bought for their wedding—the only suit he'd ever owned—and he looked handsome with a crisp white shirt against his swarthy complexion from working outside. He wore the same navy striped tie from their wedding too; it was nice to see him in something other than the work clothes he always wore—the plaid shirts and khaki-colored pants and heavy work boots but even the suit made her think of Elliott, for he was a man who always wore a suit.

Sydney unwrapped the little box, slowly tearing off the pale pink paper with petite mauve flowers, tugging at the string of ribbon to loosen it. Here was one area where Elliott could never encroach. Other than the diary he had bought her on that first Christmas, the green leather-bound book, and the leaded glass earrings, he had never given her gifts. Guiltily, she found herself annoyed at Spencer's one-upmanship in this regard; as though she didn't want a reason to side with him in the ways he was better to her than Elliott had been—ways that highlighted all that Elliott was not.

Inside was a pair of half-karat diamond earrings.

"Oh, Spencer." Sydney felt softened with vulnerability at his kindness. "They're beautiful. Oh, Spence. Thank you."

She kissed his cheek tenderly and squeezed his hand.

"They're your birthstone. They match your engagement ring," he said proudly, pointing out the same little white-gold heart-shaped setting as her ring had. "For your birthday in the second year of our marriage," he said quietly, flushing a little.

Sydney slid the diamonds onto her ears and studied herself in her compact mirror; a married woman who was cherished. The sparkle against her milk-white skin and soft dark curls added an uncustomary elegance. A flood of emotions overtook her and she rushed into the bathroom. This new image, this woman in the mirror, all grown up, with the look of pain in the reflection of her eyes, was replacing who she once was. She didn't know who she was anymore. She didn't know where she belonged. She felt to be an imposter.

Spencer was waiting patiently for her on their chocolate-brown chesterfield when she came out of the bathroom. Once again, she took in how handsome he was, sitting there in his suit, with his pants hitched up to reveal Perry Como-style argyle socks and black loafer dress shoes.

"Ready, Frenchie?" he asked, smiling up at her.

Sydney forced a smile. "All set." Then added, again. "Oh Spencer, they are just beautiful. You shouldn't have."

He kissed her cheek. "I like to spoil you."

Sydney ordered a Grasshopper Cocktail, as she always did when she and Helka came to the Cascades for lunch.

She thought again about that last time she had been here with Elliott when she had taken him to see Kakabeka Falls, and immediately sought to brush the memory from her mind when she noticed Spencer studying her as if he were wondering about what she was thinking.

Sydney didn't tell Spencer, at first, about what Dr. Montemueller had told her. She just couldn't. He hadn't said it was for sure that she couldn't carry a child, just a possibility but now they had been trying to have a baby for almost a year and a half and she still couldn't bring herself to say anything. Spencer had rescued her because of his love for her; that he had her seemed to be all he wanted and needed.

Things were fine throughout the day and while they were out together but the lovemaking was starting to take its toll. Spencer's initial tenderness and understanding had turned into a form of resentment and anger Sydney didn't fully understand. She understood enough to know, though, it had to do with her lack of affection and attentiveness toward him. She was not capable of feeling what she didn't feel or even pretending to feel something she didn't. She'd thought over time it would matter less to him but it seemed to matter more as time went on.

Some days were worse than others. When they had spent an enjoyable Sunday together, strolling around the block and having coffee while reading the newspaper to each other in the living room, everything was fine. A nice dinner followed by a glass of white wine and if Sydney was feeling amiable, they would cuddle on the couch and then make love in bed. She could never bear to have him on top of her though, to have him breathing down into her face, huffing and puffing and grunting until he was satisfied and she could barely breathe.

Other times were worse when she wasn't feeling particularly amiable or affectionate and she would turn away. Spencer seemed to tolerate it as long as he could be with her but on the bad days, she would cry. She couldn't help it. Elliott still occupied that part of her. He had possessed her, he owned her in that sense and Sydney's feelings were all tied up between her body and mind in a way she couldn't seem to comprehend or undo.

It was becoming increasingly difficult for her to conceal her tears anymore. Part of her just wanted to surrender to the truth. To live standing in her truth no matter how bad it was but she had nowhere else to go. Whether she was alone or with someone else, it would be the same, so she stayed.

On one of those nights, when she had been crying more intently than previously since she had learned she may be sterile, feeling sorry for herself, wondering what the point was of a lifetime of all this huffing and groaning, previously made bearable by the thought she might have a child and now, it seemed, only a private humiliation, a punishment inflicted by Spencer each time because of what she had done.

Spencer, it seemed, was losing patience with her as well; he'd reached the peak of his tolerance. As she lay with her back to him, trembling, trying to stop her tears, he seethed with rage behind her. Finally, he grabbed her shoulders and shook her. He pushed her back and forth and then he started to cry.

"Sydney, stop this for God's sake. What do you think of me? What do you feel for me? Am I that repulsive to you? Was he that much better? So much better than me that you are still crying for him after all this time? What is it? What was it? What did he do that made him so much better than me?"

Spencer was shouting.

"What did he have that I don't have?"

Sydney froze. She had never seen him so angry. He had never raised his voice to her. He had never laid a hand on her before. She felt scared. She felt unsafe. So she lied. She had had to think of something. Anything to make him feel better.

"It isn't that," she said. "It isn't him." She stopped and went silent.

Spencer gathered himself together. He stopped crying.

"Well, what is it then?" He waited.

Sydney stifled another cry for fear that it would enrage him again.

"It's me."

"What do you mean?" Spencer barked at her. "What do you mean by that? What is it that is you?" He sounded irritated again.

"It has to do with what Dr. Montemueller told me."

She went silent for several minutes.

"A year or so ago. Remember, when I went for all those tests?"

She hesitated. She felt afraid of Spencer. She still felt unsafe but she wanted to get this over with, no matter what the consequences would be.

"Yes, I remember," he snapped. "What's that got to do with anything?"

"Well," Sydney said, as she sat up in bed. She pulled her flannel nightgown up to her neck and plumped her pillow behind her. Her face was still wet and her eyes stung. She felt weak.

"It seems that he...that Ell...that the man I was previously to marry...it seems that he must have had others."

She was choosing her words carefully, the formality somehow a necessity to cover over the seediness of what she was about to reveal; this final blow that told her Elliott had not loved her in the way she had thought; that he was probably a man who was incapable of loving.

"Oh, come on Sydney, let's get out with it," Spencer spat at her. "I'm so tired of hearing about that bloody—that bastard. What has he got to do with it then? I thought you just told me it wasn't him."

He was raising his voice again.

"I meant that it wasn't him I was thinking about," Sydney lied again.

"Well, what exactly is it you are trying to tell me here? That Elliott Caldwell was a serial jilter?" Spencer scoffed.

Sydney still, after all this time, flinched at the sound of Elliott's name, as if in the saying of it, he might suddenly appear in the room in front of her.

"That part, I don't know about." Sydney furrowed her brow.

Until now she hadn't considered that he might have used the same ploy as a device with other women he wanted to bed. The thought of it made her feel sick to her stomach.

"No," said Sydney meekly. "No, I didn't mean that."

"Well, spit it out then."

The more passive her reaction, the more inflamed Spencer became.

"Please do tell me what it is then that this—this love of your life—" Spencer snarled, "what could he possibly have done that could still make you cry after all this time? Has he left you with a terminal illness? Is it a matter of life or death? Or has all your pining finally made you sick? Elliott Caldwell was right, isn't it time you snapped out of it?" Spencer yelled.

Sydney couldn't stop the tears streaming down her face. She sniffed and pulled a Kleenex from the box on the night table. She was quiet for a while. Spencer seemed to have worn himself down and lay back on the bed, deep in thought.

"Uh"—Sydney began, feeling empty. She just didn't know how to break this to Spencer, after everything else. She wished she hadn't begun this but there was no turning back now.

"It seems that he must have had a…a sexual…a venereal disease."

Spencer bolted up in bed. "What?"

Sydney decided she may as well finish this once and for all. She just wanted out of this place where she was stuck. A surge of anger veered up at the way Spencer was speaking to her. He, of all people.

"It isn't my fault," she wailed. "How was I to know? I was young and very foolish. It seems, well, it may even be likely, that it has left me sterile. Unable to bear any children."

Sydney broke down and cried hard. She waited for Spencer to console her, as he always did.

He was quiet for several minutes as he absorbed this shock, this final humiliating blow Elliott Caldwell had delivered to their lives.

Sydney was lost in her thoughts when she felt Spencer's foot hit her backside. She looked at him, alarmed, feeling betrayed, lost, and alone. She couldn't believe what had just happened.

Spencer kicked her again, hitting her legs hard.

"Get out. Get out of my bed. Get out of my house. Get. Just. Get. Out."

He delivered a final kick that caught her in the back.

Sydney cowered at the side of the bed and wrapped her arms in front of her and stayed there until Spencer went quiet.

Then she got up and went into the living room and sat down on the couch. She pulled her afghan blanket over the top of her legs and sat curled up there for the rest of the night. She was shaking. She felt cold and so alone. She thought about going to her parent's house but she didn't want to go back to her room there. Every time she looked into that room, at her bed, it all came back and waves of depression washed over her. She just couldn't go back there.

Once, possibly even more than once, Sydney had thought of leaving Spencer and she thought of leaving him now. To live her life honestly; to be true to herself. To live in her own truth. To not have to live with things, hide feelings, and feign feelings she did not have, to live without resentment; but in the end, she stayed.

Chapter 22
Aftermath

In the morning Sydney woke up early, still on the couch. She shivered. She looked at the clock to see the time. Five forty-five a.m. The sky was dark and rain ran down the windows. She pulled her afghan blanket over her feet but they still felt cold. Her eyes were raw from crying and lack of sleep. She heard a stifled sob and looked over to the chair on the other side of the room. Spencer was there, hunched over, wearing only his pajama bottoms, his head in his hands, fingers running through his straight sandy hair. The outline of Spencer's body was lit by the shadow of the morning. His arms were muscular from his job lifting heavy bags of grain. She found herself wondering again why she could see the beauty of Spencer's physique and yet feel no desire for him.

"What have I done?" he said, his voice practically a whisper." "What has he done? What has this Elliott Caldwell done? To you. To me. What kind of an animal am I? He's turned me into someone I didn't even know I was capable of being."

He stopped for a few moments. He leaned forward and looked closely into her eyes.

"Jealousy. Jealousy can be an evil thing, Sydney." He looked away then, afraid. "Can you forgive me?" he whispered.

She didn't speak until she'd thought hard about what to say. Deep down she knew there was no guarantee this would not happen again but there was nowhere else to put her faith.

She lifted her head but she couldn't bear to look at him. "You're only human, after all," she said. Her voice dropped to a whisper and she still couldn't look him in the eye. "Yes. Yes, I forgive you."

He moved across the room toward her and Sydney flinched involuntarily. He kneeled at her feet. His whole person had shrunk. He lay his head in her lap. She knew she should stroke his hair or place her hands on his bare shoulders but she felt repulsion toward him even more so after what he'd done. She placed one hand on his shoulder and held it there as he wept into her flannel nightgown.

After a time, he rose and took her hand. He led her back to the bedroom and she let him make love to her.

Chapter 23
A Shift in the Balance of Power

Sydney had never thought about how it might be to lose Spencer. The next day, after he left for work in the morning, she put Chopin's *Nocturne* on the record player, as she often did, and listened as she set about her morning routines. She washed the dishes and got out the leftover chicken and celery and rice and stock to make him soup for lunch. She had never learned to play the piano herself, for she had no ability, talent, or inclination for that but she drove Spencer to distraction playing those records over and over again—Kuhlau, *Sonatina Op. 55 No. 1*, Chopin's *Waltz in A Minor*, posthumous, and mostly the *Nocturne, Op. 9 No. 2*—and, therefore, Sydney waited until he had gone to work before she played them.

Most of the men who worked at the Grain Elevator took their lunch with them to work and gathered in the staff room with their metal lunch buckets, chewing on sandwiches from waxed paper wrappings, carrot and celery sticks wound tightly in the new plastic Saran Wrap, a homemade cookie or two, and milk or soup from their thermos. Spencer, though, had begun coming home on his lunch hour right after he and Sydney married, an intuitive sense driving him that she shouldn't be left alone and she was grateful for it.

She was grateful, too, for those mornings to herself, when she could be alone with her thoughts and listen to her music, take Elliott's photograph from the green diary in the top drawer of her night table, hidden under her white leather Woman's Study Bible Mum had bought for her the first Christmas after it happened, even though she'd just married Spencer a month before; Mum had known what she'd be feeling now.

To my Dearest Sydney, my first-born daughter, who I love with all my heart, I hope this will be a constant source of hope and comfort to you in these difficult days.

Sydney shoved it to the bottom of the drawer and never looked at it again. She had appreciated the gesture and memorized Mum's sentiment inside but, deep down, she knew she would never step inside another church again for as long as she lived. How could she? All those days, sitting through mass, her classes there, catechism to convert to Catholicism, all the while picturing herself and Elliott up there at the front of that church on their wedding day. It seemed to Sydney that was all she thought of now, whenever she passed by a church, the priest or minister droning on in the background, a symphony to her reverie.

In truth, even though Sydney was grateful Spencer chose to come home during his lunch hour, sometimes she would look at him, hunched over there in front of his bowl, slurping his soup off his spoon, and she would wonder who he was. Where she was. He seemed so foreign, out of place, out of context, there in his work clothes, his cap sitting silently beside him on their little grey Arborite kitchen table and they sometimes could think of nothing to say. With the radio droning away in the background, she would get up and dice a little more celery or a bit of cilantro and add it to the soup simmering on the stove, stirring it in, silence looming over the kitchen, save for the tap, tap of one of Spencer's hand-carved wooden spoons against the side of one of her Lagostina pots he had given her as a wedding gift.

Eventually, Spencer would rise, at precisely fifteen minutes before the end of his lunch hour, and announce, "Well, I should be getting back."

He stood to go, placing his khaki-colored work cap on top of his head as he bent and pecked Sydney gently on her mouth.

In the afternoons, after consuming a lunch she had prepared to try to please him, he would return to the Grain Elevator, and the afternoons were better for Sydney.

Kiidumae

She would tend to her garden in the summer or to her chores in winter, sewing birthday and Christmas gifts for their nieces and nephews, thawing a chunk of venison or a bear roast from the freezer to prepare for dinner, the stores from Spencer's hunting trips to Dorion in the fall.

It now seemed Spencer had always been with her, from the day they first had met. She thought back to when they were in grade eight and everything seemed so different when they were just friends. She thought back too, to the day they'd run into each other at Current River, soon after he'd returned from the war and he'd flipped open his wallet to show her he was still carrying around her school picture.

She remembered, too, that sense of power she had felt over him, knowing how he felt about her and she remembered how profound it was; as if the universe were giving her a message—dictating its advance warning to where her true destiny lay.

The other night, when Spencer kicked her from the bed, his voice brittle with bitterness, she had felt a temporary loss of that power and, for the first time, knew that it was not inexhaustible. It was possible to lose Spencer and this realization frightened her almost as much as when she had lost Elliott.

This knowledge proved to right the balance of power in their relationship. She continued with her morning rituals while Spencer was at work, studying Elliott's photograph and doing her chores to the sound of Chopin's *Nocturne* floating through the house but, when he came home, there was a newfound sense of respect. Respect of her need of him and of what it was to be loved completely by someone. An unconditional love she now knew could be broken if boundaries were not kept.

A shift in the rhythm of their love-making grew out of this respect and Sydney no longer cried, or even felt as if she wanted to cry. Her emotions were in check, a sense of survival muted her deepest feelings and she held her breath as Spencer pushed up and down on top of her, exhaling afterward, with a self-satisfied smile, knowing she was learning to live with it and she had landed upon the right balance, the rhythm needed to stay where she was.

"Indecision is a decision," Papa always said when she'd asked him if he thought she should marry Spencer after he proposed, afraid it would destroy their friendship.

In the week following what was to have been Sydney's wedding day, she had immediately taken an extended leave of absence from her job at the hospital laundry. Just the thought of what she should say, or picturing Chuffy's father's endearing look of sympathy, or hearing in her mind the snickers and "I told you so's" from the other girls she worked with, would cause her to redden with shame. Aunt Bess had stayed on for a spell, after she'd come down from Winnipeg for the wedding, and taught Sydney how to sew. After she'd left, Sydney spent most of her days, alone in her room, reading, and she'd started walking Deedee to and from school, to get out of the house.

Despite Mum's fears of her becoming a spinster, Sydney had been invited out on several dates as soon as the other boys knew she was available again but she no longer trusted men and spurned them all. She was never sure what they were truly thinking of her after they'd heard all the rumors.

"Men are only interested in one thing," Mum nagged at her, no longer trusting them herself either. So, in the summer months, Sydney had sat in the double canopy swing in the backyard, reading.

Spencer seemed to know well enough to keep his distance from her for a while and Sydney would often see him there, sitting on the front porch with his parents or standing inside looking out their living room window, smoking a cigarette and watching her as she sat on the swing in the back garden.

"When you're ready, Frenchie, just let me know and we'll take a drive or go for a walk along the river," he'd said as if he were holding vigil for her. Often, she wished he'd go out on dates with other girls and quit hovering over her so; but there he was, as patient as an old dog.

Despite all this, Sydney was still surprised when he'd asked her to marry him and even more surprised when she found herself saying yes. She pondered Papa's words now and wondered whether love really is just a decision—that maybe this was all love ever really was.

Chapter 24
Wedding Bells

My Dearest Helka,
  Of course, I do hope you are enjoying your getaway in Niagara Falls, a well-deserved honeymoon for you and Will; but you are away at just the worst possible time. Oh, Helka, it's all so very awful, you will not believe it. I know when you read the enclosed newspaper clipping you will understand what I mean.

Wedding Bells May Save Attempted Murder Charge for Nineteen-Year-Old Girl read the headline in the Midland-Penetanguishene Mirror. Sydney's mouth fell open when she'd read it— it was Francine, Francine Napier. She read on. Francine had stabbed her fiancé, Milton Diaz, in the stomach with a kitchen knife. She came home from work and found him with another girl on his lap, a visiting friend, and he kissed the girl on the lips, in front of Francine, spurning her into a jealous rage.

Sydney had felt a wave of nausea and dizziness when she read the newspaper article. "Come quickly, you've got to read this," she'd called out to Spencer, sitting in the garden sipping a beer, enjoying the fruits of his labor. "There's been an accident," she cried. "It's all just so horrible."

Sydney read on. There was a quote, from the preliminary hearing, Milton Diaz saying "Yes, we still plan to get married, we love each other." There was a witness, a friend, who was visiting at the time, who had seen Francine take the knife from the kitchen drawer in a distraught state but hadn't actually witnessed the stabbing, so it was all circumstantial, his word against Francine's and a husband isn't required to testify against his wife unless he chooses to, so if the wedding took place before the final court hearing, Francine could be acquitted.

Sydney had known Francine long enough to know she wasn't completely stable but she never thought she was capable of this. She continued her letter to Helka.

Oh, Helka, I always did think Francine Napier was a little silly, a little boy-crazy but no one, no one deserves this, and to think she asked me to be her maid of honor at her wedding. I was only going to accept because I knew she had asked two other girls already and they both refused. Francine's letter, asking me, was sitting on top of my dresser when I saw the newspaper article. A friend of Spencer's sent it to us. I was still deliberating over whether or not I wanted to make the drive back and forth between Port Arthur and Penetanguishene for rehearsals. Now that I've seen this, I feel sick. I know in all good conscience I will not be able to be her maid of honor.

Oh God, Helka, after I first read the newspaper article I sat down on the couch and started thinking. I sat there for a long time until the room started to get dark. I needed to get up and go to the bathroom, but I just continued sitting there. I felt stunned, repelled—that feeling of sinking shock when you find out that someone is not what they seemed. When I really thought about it though, reflecting back on some of Francine's behavior, I shouldn't have been all that surprised. How is it that sometimes we don't see what's right in front of us; maybe all of our relationships are only illusions of how we think people are, of how we see them or choose to see them? Well, anyway, truth be told, given Francine Napier's taste in men and given the family of her fiancé—one of three brothers, only two now left after one shot himself in the head playing a game of Russian Roulette with the other two—it was only a matter of time until something like this happened.

The thing is, Helka, the main reason for my letter is really not to do with Francine at all though—of course, I immediately contacted her and begged off being her maid of honor, making up an excuse of another family wedding; but we had all heard the rumors—that Milton Diaz was bringing home girls from the pub, coming in late, sneaking them into his parents' spare room, and all the while engaged to Francine, three months pregnant with his child and so, none of this was a complete surprise. All I could think of though—dear Helka, I do wish you were here so I could talk to you—all I could think was it could have been me. Here I am thinking to myself what a darned fool Francine Napier is but I remembered the time, that night I saw Betty Blackwell coming out of Elliott's apartment. I didn't know why and I realized this could just as easily have been me.

I thought of my dear Spencer, who would never contemplate such a thing, even though he does not have the benefit of the complete and utter devotion from me that we all know Francine has for Milton Diaz and my Spencer is so good, kind, and trustworthy and would never in a million years treat me such. All this time, here's me, feeling sorry for myself, Helka, and it could have been so much worse. So much worse, if I had married Elliott. If I had married that slippery man, Elliott, who is to say he wouldn't have done the same such things as Milton Diaz, or what he was capable of?

But, oh dear, I do not want to think about myself. I realize that is all I have ever done since Elliott left and, possibly, if it wasn't for the plight of Francine, it might have been all I ever could do and it would make me bitter, lonesome and useless. Helka, what's that saying? 'All the tears that have fallen from my eyes seem now to have sharpened my ability to see.'

If you were here right now, I would arrange for us to go straight to the Cascades and order a Grasshopper Cocktail and toast to the future—to our wonderful, blessed lives. When you return, we must do exactly that. Suddenly, everything feels so bright and alive, just to think of how it all could have been so much worse.

Kiidumae

Now, I must sign off, as my next letter is going to be to Aunt Bessie. I've been to the Changes Consignment Boutique on South May Street to see about making some of my designs to sell, the ones Aunt Bess always said I was so good at—and I'm going to ask her to ship me more boxes of clothes and buttons. Oh Helka, I can hardly wait. I just want to kiss the grass and my own hand and lift it to the sky.

Please, do hurry on home here, Helka, before I absolutely burst.

Hugs and Kisses,
Sydney

Chapter 25
Making a Life

Sydney set her coffee cup on the arm of her Adirondack chair and walked to the garden shed in the corner of the yard. It was early spring and Spencer was busy working the ground to plant potatoes. The sleeves of his khaki shirt were rolled up to his upper arms. His muscles tensed each time he dug the shovel back into the earth. She'd been watching him for a while, deep in concentration at his task, the sun shining down on him, through the golden strands of his hair. She got a small shovel from the shed and walked over and stood next to him and smiled. He looked over at her. She dug her shovel in. It only just penetrated the surface at first.

The ground was still a bit frosty beneath the top layer. She looked at Spencer again, sheepishly, and dug in harder this time, pushing down on the shovel with her rain boots. He leaned his arm on his shovel handle and studied her, looking both pleased and surprised then turned and began to dig.

She had seen another side to him recently when he broke down and cried as he talked to Mum about them being unable to have children. It had moved her in a way she found surprising. For the most part, though, their lives evolved into a series of routines that marked the passage of time. He no longer seemed to blame her and an unspoken truce evolved between them—she no longer spurned him in the matrimonial bed, her previous repulsion now turned to a form of comfort in the familiarity of their lovemaking which, in itself, had turned into a form of routine. He still chastised himself for his transgression in losing himself to his temper. He'd retreat to his workshop in the basement with his fishing flies and implements of carpentry, if even the slightest inkling of these feelings arose again.

In spring, they planted their garden together, happily chattering to each other, the transistor on the back porch tuned to CKPR, the station that played the cheerful music that kept them moving as they strolled through the yard, loading debris into the wheelbarrow with matching gloved hands. Sammy and Sadie, the Samoyed Huskies Spencer had brought home for her last Christmas, slept in the sun on the concrete sidewalk.

They made a trip back to the camp at Dorion every May long weekend to open it up again for the season, shaking the dust from all the old woven rugs on the floor, placing clean linens on the beds, a bouquet of wild spring flowers on the wooden table where they shared a bowl of Sydney's homemade soup served with crusty buns.

Spring turned into summer where evenings were spent in their sunny garden, sipping coffee or tea; on weekends Spencer would have his beer. Together they admired the growth of the garden, starting with sticks poking up with the names of the vegetables on them; later in the summer, she balanced a bowl of unshelled peas on her lap, her feet resting on Sammy's and Sadie's backs, hucking away. Sydney had always detested the sight of yards with tacky garden gnomes but, year by year, the collection of frogs that Spencer gave her accumulated around the garden, in corners, at the entrance to the back door as lion's head pillars and, over time, she even developed a fondness for them.

Summer nights they ate salads together in the garden and, on weekends, Helka and Dr. Will Kirby and their five children came for backyard barbeques—simple fare of hamburgers and hotdogs, potato salad, and Sydney's homemade baked beans. They played peek-a-boo and hide and go seek with Helka and Will's children, winking at them and tickling under their arms when they were caught, with a twinkle in their eyes, and the children laughed and ran off. Occasionally, Sydney and Spencer took the children for a night or two, to give Helka and Will a break, feeding them prunes for breakfast, rubbing them down with big thick terry towels after their baths then, loading them in the truck in their pajamas, Spencer drove them to the Dairy Queen on the corner of Cumberland Street for an ice cream cone before bed. Sometimes, after they left, Sydney detected the sadness there, in Spencer's eyes, the void in their lives that could never be filled and she burned deep with guilt.

One year, on her birthday, Spencer came home with a pair of canaries in a cage and set it up in the kitchen, next to Sammy's and Sadie's bowls, trying to fill that void Sydney suspected. The birds were there, waiting for her in the mornings when she lifted the cover off their cage and replenished their water and birdseed, always singing. So she'd named them Tweetie and Peep.

Come fall, they picked their winter stores from the garden and Sydney busied herself canning various fruits and berry jams, cucumber dill pickles, corn relish, and baked zucchini loaves, while Spencer smoked and canned the Chinook salmon he'd caught and frozen at the camp at Dorion in the summer.

While Spencer was at work Sydney's daily salads evolved into soups and stews and homemade baked beans and casseroles. From a carefully detailed calendar that hung on the wall in her sewing room, she made clothes for each of their nieces and nephews, on their birthday and every Christmas. On weekends Spencer hunted back at the Camp—deer and bear, mostly, and together they packaged and labeled the venison and other cuts of meat and loaded them, in date order, into the basement freezer that Spencer had surprised her with one year just before Christmas.

River of Forgiveness

When the snow started to fall, Spencer no longer made the trek home for lunch. Sydney came to cherish those times, alone for the entire day, tending to chores, listening to Chopin's Nocturne on the Victrola in the living room, making dinner as she sang to herself in the kitchen.

Some days Helka came for lunch; others she went to Helka's. They'd share a glass of white wine as they gossiped about the neighbors and spoke to each other of their marriages but Sydney found the interruption and constant demands for attention from the children tiring and so, over time, these visits dwindled until Helka's children were older, off busily engaged in their own activities.

"To fall in love passionately," Sydney told Helka on one of those afternoons in the garden, one particularly hot day, when they'd had a few extra glasses and were feeling quite tipsy, a combination of the heat and the wine, "is to lose yourself to someone, to partially die, until one part dies so that the other may live. Better to learn to love someone slowly, like this, a slow awakening of tenderness that brings you to life, flourishes your very being, like a flower being watered, where Saturdays are not spent anguishing over what the other person is feeling."

In late November, on Grey Cup Sunday, when the stores were the least busy and everything was on sale, Sydney and Helka went to the Hudson's Bay together and spent the day Christmas shopping, having lunch and tea at the Bonnie's-Team Room, midway through the day.

Sometimes the subject of adoption came up as she and Spencer watched movies or spent time in the garden but Sydney had a preconceived notion of adopted children. She believed such a child would come with its own load of troubles. Spencer was afraid the mother might want them back again, later, and couldn't bear the thought of such a heartbreak.

Then, suddenly, Mum died. Her weak heart finally gave out one day while she stood mixing her fruitcakes for Christmas. Papa found her on the kitchen floor, the oven preheating. Afterward, somehow the pressure to bear children wasn't there anymore. So the months turned into years and Sydney's fortieth birthday was around the corner and time then seemed to have run out and she felt too old.

Deep down, Sydney feared she'd wasted her life and was wasting her life now. She didn't always feel this fear; it came to her occasionally, and when it did it stopped her cold. After an hour, or a day, and sometimes after a week of grinding malaise, it would slip away again at the prospect of a wedding or a baby shower or a Christmas party to attend. She supposed everyone had those feelings from time to time and so she paid as little attention to them as she could. She never forced the issue of adoption on Spencer. She knew some men—men such as her husband—wanted to raise their own babies, not another man's child. Her own maternal instinct, it seemed had abandoned her at the same time as had her one first true love.

Chapter 26
Turning Forty

On Sydney's fortieth birthday Spencer held a party for her in the backyard. It was a cool, sunny spring day and the mauve and yellow crocuses in the planter box under the kitchen window were already in bloom. The party had been a surprise. Spencer kept it simple so he could plan it without her knowing, stashing cases of soft drinks and beer down in the fridge next to his workshop. Spencer's sister-in-law made dozens of little sandwiches—salmon, egg salad, ham, and peanut butter and jam for the children.

Spencer ordered a special cake down at Sweet Dreams Catering & Bakery on Cumberland Street—chocolate, Sydney's favorite, and large enough to hold the forty candles. He wheeled it out on a TV tray as Sydney sat in her Adirondack chair with Sammy and Sadie at her feet. Will and Helka and her five children, Papa, and Chuffy and Maisie with their three, Deedee and her four, and a few neighbors sat around her on folding chairs in a semi-circle. Helka lit the candles while Spencer popped open bottles of bubbly—not real champagne—Mateus Rosé sparkling wine.

"Make a wish," Helka said, "before you blow the candles out."

"You expect me to blow all of those out in one breath?" Sydney laughed.

She sucked in her breath and tried to think of a wish. She exhaled again. She couldn't think that fast. The only thing she had ever wished for in her life that she hadn't been able to have was Elliott Caldwell, this, and the ability to have children. She wondered about Elliott now. His lack of integrity had become more clear to her over the years, the memories and passions more distant.

Spencer was true blue. She knew he would never hurt her. That he had no secrets. That with her good and simple husband what you saw was what you got.

Spencer plunked down in the chair next to her and struck a match to relight the three candles that the breeze had blown out then lit a cigarette for himself. He let out a wheeze and a cough as he inhaled and looked at the half-melted candles.

"Frenchie, are you going to hurry up and blow those candles out, or are you planning on burning the house down?"

She blew on the candles as everyone sang *Happy Birthday* and, after five tries, all the candles were out.

"Five years, Sydney, five years until you get your wish," Helka said. "What did you wish for?" She leaned in close and whispered into Sydney's ear.

"I can't tell you, or else it will be bad luck and my wish won't come true. You know that."

"Oh, don't be silly, Sydney," Helka scolded. "Here, knock on wood first then."

Sydney smiled. She knocked three times on the arm of her chair and her knuckle hit a soft spot that was beginning to rot and the end broke off. She pulled Helka close.

"Forty more, I wished for forty more birthdays, just like this one."

Spencer overheard and kissed Sydney's nose, over top of a few freckles that had cropped up under the early spring sun. He rested his hand on top of hers, in his easy, smiling way, then squeezed her fingers and lifted them to his mouth and kissed them. Sydney saw a glisten of wetness in the corners of his eyes.

"Thank you, Spencer." Sydney kissed him on the lips. His mouth tasted of a mix of tobacco and sparkling wine. He reached for her hand and she reached for his in return. Their guests clapped and cheered and Spencer rose and circled the garden, refilling everyone's glass, while Sydney and Helka cut the cake and passed out the pieces on paper plates.

They ate their cake, as Sydney pointed out the shoots and buds to Helka in the garden. They drank in their friendship and the warm sun on their skin along with mugs of freshly brewed coffee. Helka was only half listening as Sydney spoke, "…and have a look at those tulips planted along the side of the house…"

"Hey, what was your second wish?" she interrupted. "When you cut the cake?" Helka leaned in close again and rubbed up against Sydney's shoulder.

Sydney started to laugh until she was laughing so hard, she had to hold her stomach.

"What's so funny? C'mon, tell me," Helka said.

Sydney laughed. "Remember old Mrs. Abercrombie, from homeroom?" she asked.

"Sort of, not too well though. I remember she was very pregnant, just a few weeks away from giving birth, by the end of the year. She was quite huge with the baby but had a pretty good girth on her, to begin with. Why? What on earth does this have to do with your wish? Did you wish for a baby, Sydney?"

"No, don't be so silly. It's just the way you said 'hey,' when you asked me my wish. Remember Mrs. Abercrombie always used to say to Tom Coates, 'Don't say hay, I'm not a horse.' whenever he called out to her. We got a detention once because we started laughing so hard the first time she'd said that."

Helka started to laugh too. "Tell me what your other wish was or I'll have to spray you with the hose over there," she teased.

"Helka, you are just too darned nosey."

"Ah, c'mon."

"Oh, all right. 'Little Pitchers Have Big Ears' as Mum used to say. If you truly want to know, I wished that you and I would always be together. I wished for our friendship never to end."

Helka was speechless for a few moments, caught completely off guard. Tears filled her eyes.

"Well now," Helka said, clearing a lump from her throat, "you know that's just not going to be humanly possible, now is it? Since all human relationships have a beginning and an ending. It's either separation or death, I'm afraid."

Sydney was quiet for some time and finally said, "I just can't bear to think of it."

Helka put her arm around Sydney's shoulders and squeezed tight and they stayed that way until it was starting to get dark and they felt chilled.

"Time to go in now you girls," Spencer said, with a wink.

River of Forgiveness

Chapter 27
The Kind of Bird I Am

She'd sensed it as soon as he had his first nose bleed, but still, she was left with a feeling of disbelief after he died. Those last months, when Spencer had quit drinking and smoking, had quit retiring alone to the basement at night with his transistor radio and his salmon flies and trout flies—an occupation that, along with his jars of carved wooden spoons, he had, in those last months, quit making, the flies and spoons given away to everyone he knew, and now it all seemed pointless, "a bit too little, too late," as Mum would have said.

    These hobbies, Spencer replaced with daily walks to the 7-Eleven to purchase confectionery, ice cream, newspapers, magazines and, later, Wintario lottery tickets, not for himself, of course, because money never had mattered to him much. He'd never had any ambition beyond his foreman's position at the Grain Elevator—he was as successful as he ever wanted to be, he said, "as he had been the day he'd married his wife." He'd been frugal, though, to the last, even a bit of a tightwad, Deedee had called him, and a saver, but he wanted in those last days to leave Sydney with more. He had a life insurance policy and a good pension from all of his years at the Elevator but he somehow wanted to prove, in death, her life with him had been worth it.

Forty-nine was still young, way too young to die, as Helka and Spencer's brother Alfred and everyone else would later say. Sydney had somehow always pictured him going last when she sat at the table drinking wine with Helka and Spencer and his brother after the sharing of a meal in one of their kitchens and such thoughts would come to her.

Over the years, Sydney had often wondered and even fantasized about how her life would look if Spencer died before his time and now she knew this was her punishment for her selfishness. In the early years, it was part of her way out, imagining some terrible accident at the grain elevator or a hunting mishap that might leave her free to believe that it was her marriage that had kept Elliott Caldwell away and that he might now return to her at this news of her husband's death.

"Did I honestly ever love Spencer?" Sydney asked Helka after she'd scattered his ashes in Current River.

"Of course you did. Else you wouldn't have married him. There are so many different ways to love."

In those last months, leading up to his death, they hadn't spoken of it much. Spencer, always practical, saw no point in dwelling on the inevitable. Instead of cooking, at lunchtime they hopped in the truck and drove to the Cascades at Kakabeka Falls or the Ruby Moon Café on Court Street, breathing in the fresh air as they rode, enjoying the sun coming in through the open windows.

"I worked my whole life, Frenchie," Spencer said, on one of those ventures. "And now I'm just a statistic. I won't even collect the national average of fourteen months payments from the Canada Pension Plan."

"Not everything's about money," Sydney scolded, but she had understood what he meant. That was when she'd first asked herself what the point of life really was.

Afterward, she told Helka she felt as though she'd wasted her life. She said she'd sat across from Spencer at the Ruby Moon the previous week and saw how thin he was getting. His face was wrinkled and pale and his sideburns were almost completely grey; but when she'd looked at him again, more closely, she could still see the old Spencer, sitting on the picnic blanket at Current River, or standing in the river at Dorion with his fishing rod—so at peace. Content. What would she do without him? He was her whole life and she hadn't even really chosen him.

Kiidumae

After Spencer was too ill to go out and needed to rest in bed most of the day, Sydney cared for him at home. On the good days, she pressed on his forehead with a cool cloth with the bedroom drapes drawn, sunlight filtering in through the cream-colored cotton, and she read to him.

"I declare, Frenchie," Spencer would say, "You finally got me to read. Had to lock me up or immobilize me first," he chuckled. He enjoyed being read to, though. The soft sound of her voice, speaking in hushed tones beside him, her lovely voice he'd known ever since childhood and he told her he wanted to etch that sound into his mind forever. "To eternity, I should say," he teased after she'd read him *From Here to Eternity*.

She'd read him books she thought he would like, mostly Ernest Hemingway's fiction stories of fishing and hunting but, after a few weeks, he said, "Read me one of yours, Frenchie. I like it when I can hear the love in your voice." And she'd read to him then from *Wuthering Heights*, from *Gone with the Wind*, and Jane Austen's novels. She skipped out the humorous parts because when he laughed it set him to coughing and she couldn't bear to hear it or to see the blood splay out onto his handkerchief.

They talked, too. They spoke of their childhood days together, they reminisced about the day they'd taken off their clothes to splash in the puddle. They spoke too of what their unborn children would have looked like, of what they would have named them and Spencer said how he wished he'd had a little girl who looked just like her, one with beautiful big brown eyes and dark curly hair—another little hand to hold.

They both conceded though, their life together had been good, for the most part, they'd been as happy as likely anyone ever could be and how Sadie and Sammy were the same as having two children anyway. When it got close to the end, Sydney told him she wished she'd married him sooner and she wished he'd been her first and only love. She said this even though she didn't quite mean it, even though she knew she'd likely never have settled if she hadn't needed him; but she told him this because she knew it was what he wanted to hear. When she saw Spencer's eyes flood with tears and grasp at her hand, holding it against his chest, she'd even wished that it was true.

On the bad days, Spencer was too weak to talk and so she would let him rest, puttering in the kitchen to make his meals, avoiding acidic fruit juices and spicy foods that might sting his throat. His mouth was dry after his radiotherapy and made it difficult for him to swallow food, so she made him soup broths and kept a pitcher of water next to his bed. She cringed when she heard the rattling sound in his chest, knowing his blood was coming up with it and knowing too, with each exhale, he was worsening.

In those final days, Sydney felt so much tenderness for Spencer as he lay dying that it filled her with remorse and made her feel as though she'd squandered their life to emotional trivialities. She vowed to live in the present moment for as much time as they had left. As it got closer to the end, she realized, too, she had wallowed in a bygone past that could never be recaptured and yet, there he always was, Spencer, before her very eyes, filled with love for her and she now knew it was enough; she no longer wanted for more.

After he was gone, Helka told her she needed to reconnect with herself. She had to start looking inside herself and at the world around her, instead of at just one person, counting on that magic someone to make her happy.

She spent nights in front of the television crying and eating Bridge Mixture. The pain in losing Spencer took her back to that time of grieving after Elliott left her. She brought out her mementos of that first love and studied his photograph for clues as she listened to Chopin's Nocturne. In the mornings she sat alone in her living room, still wearing her nightgown and an old brown cardigan, and took to wearing Spencer's old work socks for slippers as she read through the entries in her green leather diary.

Sydney wondered where Elliott was now. *Has he waited for me? Did he go back to his wife and children? Or did he marry again, maybe to someone else?* She briefly considered hiring a private investigator to find him but this last thought held her back. She was over fifty years old now. Spencer had been a year younger than that when he died and the thought of being widowed made her feel even older. She still looked remarkably youthful, Helka told her though. Still with the same short curled hairstyle, not even half turned to grey, a flattering salt-and-pepper look that accented her brown eyes and her complexion, rosy and tanned from working in the garden and she was still petite, with only a few rolls of flesh around her middle.

When she read the green diary, she still saw herself as she'd looked back then, on what was to have been her wedding day but her hazel eyes were dulled a little now, with pain and the first signs of cataracts, and her twinkle was no longer visible—she was altered. No, she would not want Elliott to see her this way; but she could still go back to him, in her reverie; when she listened to the music, it took her back there to him, in her mind and her heart.

She kept busy during the long days cooking for herself, tidying the house, feeding, and bathing and walking her newly adopted little dog, Ellie, a Chow Chow—the lap dog she'd always wanted, just an excuse for a dog, Spencer would say—keeping up the yard in summer, weeding the vegetable garden, raking in the fall, shoveling snow in the winter but she'd lost her spark when Spencer died. She could feel it. It was akin to finding out how a story or a sad book ends and you wish you could go back to the beginning, except it was her life. So much emphasis on love and which was the right love, now she had no one, neither of them was left.

One day while visiting with Papa and Deedee, things changed. Deedee's husband, long plagued by a bad heart, had suffered a stroke years earlier, right before Mum died, so she and her husband and four children had moved in with Papa, to help take care of him. The day Sydney visited, still burdened by these thoughts of Spencer and Elliott, Deedee found an old apron in the kitchen drawer from when she was a girl.

Inside the pocket was Reginald Hunt's business card. He was the private investigator who'd come to their door looking for Elliott a week after their wedding was to have been. His business card was still there from that afternoon all those years ago. Neither of them could believe it. Sydney was feeling better now these days and was healthy and fit from her walks with Ellie. Suddenly, she wanted to know. She wanted to know where he was. She wanted to see him.

When she got home, she called the number on Reginald Hunt's business card, fully expecting him not to be there, for the number to be no longer in service, for his business to have long been closed; but he was still there. He'd sold the business and was training a new investigator and only took on certain work himself now, part-time where he didn't have to go too far from home. He said he vaguely remembered who she was. Sydney surmised he really may not have but it didn't matter to her anyway and, as it was, it wasn't long before she found him.

She'd booked an appointment to talk to Reginald Hunt to see what he thought and, when she walked into his office two days later, he shuffled out to the lobby to greet her, heartily shaking her hand. He was graying and stooped over but something in his dark brown eyes remained the same as she'd remembered him—a mix of steely hardness and compassion that had softened a little with age. He seemed to already know why she'd come, as if he'd half expected her all these years and, to Sydney's relief, offered her no sympathy or remorse, only a twinkle of excited anticipation at receiving more work.

    Reginald Hunt came to her door a few weeks after she'd been to see him and asked if he could come in and sit down. She made a pot of tea and her hands were shaking so much from the anticipation and excitement the teacups rattled on the saucers when she set them down. He pulled a newspaper clipping from his briefcase and handed it to her. It was dated just a few months earlier. He looked down at the floor as she read it.

Man Dies in London House Fire

Robert Holley's last act on earth was one of bravery.

Holley, 63, who perished in a fire that ripped through his home early Monday morning, called to his wife and son to leave the house as the fire raged out of control.

He yelled up at them, "Get out! Get out!" said his son Alexander.

The blaze that gutted the historic home at 598 Dufferin Avenue was the first fatal fire in London in 1979.

The noxious smoke and flames may have taken Holley's life, but his disabled wife, Elsa, and disabled son Benjamin, 35, who has Louis Parkinson's disease, were able to break through a window and scamper onto the roof of the front porch of the house where they were rescued by firefighters.

They were both taken to St. Joseph's Hospital to recover from smoke inhalation and released later in the day.

"He was the kindest man you'd ever meet and had a smile for everyone," Alexander Holley said. His eyes burdened with tears, he described his parents' loving relationship and how they didn't join clubs, nor do much outside the house.

"They were each other's hobby. They were two peas in a pod. It's so hard on mom because they loved each other very much."

The article went on to tell the details of the fire and more about their lives. At the top of the story was a photograph of Elsa, now blondish grey, sitting in a wheelchair, one of her sons in a wheelchair next to her, the other standing behind them with a hand on each shoulder. He looked so much like Elliott that it made her heart catch and her eyes fill with tears. Inset was a small photograph of Elliott, still the same, smiling and older-looking, with a full head of salt-and-pepper hair, like hers.

"Can you leave me please," she asked Reginald Hunt. He left, soundlessly. Sydney gasped and sobbed into her hand until she feared she might vomit from the grief.

When she'd first read the newspaper article, she thought the story was from London, England but when she read it again, she noticed it was from a newspaper in London, Ontario. *So, he came back. Back to Canada. Or he never left. And never once did he call me or need or want to see me.* It sounded as if he'd had a happy life and marriage, other than the health of his wife and son; however, he had children, something of which he'd robbed her and Spencer. *Better that he's dead*, she thought then instantly wanted to take it back. If he'd been still alive, it would have made no difference. After all the years she'd continued to love him. Her stomach ached with loss and longing, for the part of her that was missing, but she no longer even knew what it was.

There was a certain stoicism in the acceptance of one's fate, which appealed to Sydney. She abandoned the wearing of any make-up, jewelry or lipstick. She abandoned her lacey blouses for sweatshirts and men's-styled button-up shirts, skirts and dresses for trousers, and dress shoes for men's-style lace-up boots. In her solitude, she awoke alone and slept alone; she turned the stereo up loud with her Chopin. At times she found she was muttering to herself, justifying the change in her imagining of herself, explaining to anyone who might enquire about these changes in her, "Well, that's just the kind of bird I am."

She threw away most of Spencer's trout flies and wooden spoons, along with boxes of work socks and boots and frayed flannel shirts. She held a yard sale in the driveway and got rid of the entire collection of frogs Spencer had bought her over the years.

The dampness, the damp sadness, soaked into the concrete walls in the basement and into the dark wood paneling at Dorion and filled her with foreboding. She gave away Spencer's hunting rifle to the young fellow next door, Helen's husband Tommy, sold the camp. She painted the walls in the basement a bright white and installed white laminate cupboards to organize her laundry items and cleaning implements. Nothing, though, took away the sadness that permeated through the next nine years of her life, a life that turned from being alone to loneliness, a loneliness that left her no longer able to see that it mattered anymore if she got up and got dressed in the mornings.

Sometimes, Helka would take an afternoon away from her busy life with her children and grandchildren and intrude into Sydney's self-annihilation. She'd throw a clean blouse and pair of trousers onto the bed and order Sydney into them. Helka banged the mustiness and the scent of age from Sydney's cushions on the couch where she spent most of her day, taking them out into the sunshine to air, while she put on a fresh pot of coffee to percolate.

Helka couldn't help but notice the shrine Sydney kept in the corner of the living room—a tattered photograph of Elliott Caldwell in a frame on the end table next to the oval framed picture of Spencer in his army uniform, the old Victrola record player, next to a pile of classical records, an old grey sock.

"Sydney Elizabeth Archambault-Frye, I want you to put Elliott Caldwell out of your mind and heart forever, as he told you to do in his letter." Helka told her at the time. She didn't have the heart to say anything else or to throw the items out. Ultimately, the only thing that would always be there for Sydney was the world and all that was in it, with all that is offered. Life. Life itself. That was what was Sydney's friend—not these memories and meaningless trinkets. This, Helka knew, Sydney needed to discover for herself.

Sydney put on a front as Helka left, forcing a smile from her lip-sticked mouth. Helka shook her head sadly in dismay on her way out the door. As soon as she was gone the blouse and slacks were replaced by the old flannel nightgown and Sydney's old sweater and socks.

Everyone was worried but what Sydney did next was completely unexpected. "I knew she was depressed, yes, but I would have never expected this," Helka told Deedee later.

Chapter 28
Fire!

It was Deedee who the neighbors called after the fire department when they saw the flames licking out of Sydney's kitchen window. Helen from next door ran over and instinctively went for the hose at the side of the house, spraying in through the broken kitchen window. She was a hero, the fire chief told her.

"Or, I guess, actually, a heroine," he corrected himself.

Deedee's eyes were wide with terror when she came in through the back door and collapsed onto a kitchen chair. She had begun, in age, to resemble Mum, Sydney thought, in appearance and theatrics, a tendency to melodrama.

"Sydney, what happened? Whatever were you thinking? Where was your mind at?"

Sydney plumped down in the chair next to Deedee and looked over at the charred remains of her green and white curtains. She started to get up, to fix things up but felt too drained and exhausted to complete the action. Her eyes were hot with tears and stung from the heavy smoke that hung in the air.

Sydney had been thinking of that fortieth birthday party. It was her birthday today, her sixtieth now and no one had remembered. Or, if they had, they hadn't said. She stood in front of the stove, looking out the window into the garden and she could picture everyone there, Spencer squeezing her arm then giving her a wink and she winking back.

She had been turning on the stove to reheat some of her baked beans for dinner. Something about the memory crossed over into her mind and she was back there, at her fortieth, a time when people still loved and cared for her. She'd reached for the matches and lit one and turned on the stove and held the match to the front right element. Her mind was seeing the old gas stove that she and Spencer had back then, at the camp at Dorion then she kept picturing Elliott and how he had died, and the match flared up as it touched the red coil. She threw it on the lit burner, again confusing it, somehow, with that old propane stove she and Spencer had when they were first married. Her memories were often clouded now—confused as to order or time—what was then and what was now. What was Spencer and what was Elliott, and somewhere in those memories was the resentment and the anger she'd had to quell, with nowhere to channel it. She began to relive it and was no longer clear what was real. Deep down she knew on some level that she had known exactly what she was doing. She had now, as then, wanted to do something, anything, to blow it all up, to get out of this untenable place where she was stuck.

The flame likely would have gone out but a light early evening breeze blew in through the open kitchen window and Sydney's green and white gingham curtains fanned out over the stove. She'd thrown the match and it landed, of all places, in one of the folds in the curtains and caught the flame. A hollow boom reverberated through the kitchen and off the walls as the stove and the curtains melded together into a blazing inferno.

Sydney stood at the window, watching the fire until it was too hot to stand so close. Sirens screamed down Penfold Street and stopped in front of number 189. Sydney hadn't done anything to try to stop the flames. As she'd stood, staring into the blaze, there was a part of her that knew, again, that somehow she had done it intentionally. Some infernal act of rage—rage at Spencer for abandoning her, just as Elliott Caldwell had done by dying, and everyone else, Helen and Deedee and Helka and Will, abandoning her on her birthday. She'd gone back into her head with Elliott Caldwell and just stayed there as the fire rose over the curtains.

Later, she'd felt comforted, even though she had stopped pretending to care, as the police car drove her to the acute care center near Current River. Deedee was at her side, holding the teddy bear that had belonged to Sydney as a child, one that Aunt

Bess had bought her when she'd gone to live with them, which Deedee had brought along believing that it might comfort her. On Sydney's lap, in a cardboard box, she held all of her prized possessions—the framed picture of Spencer in his army uniform, the record player, the album of Chopin's Nocturnes, the ragged photograph of Elliott Caldwell tucked inside the front cover of her green leather diary, a yellowed copy of e.e. cummings' *50 Poems*. One clings to an escape world, she'd heard, when they need to get away from the real world, away from the makings of their day-to-day existence.

Chapter 29
Back to the River

She noticed the cross hanging on a nail on top of a strip of faded blue and white floral wallpaper for the first time later that evening when Nurse came in with a sedative. When she did see it, it seemed that was all she could see, everywhere, from every angle in the room.

"Take it down," Sydney commanded when she saw it.

Of course, Nurse complied and sheepishly took it away.

When Helka came to see her in the acute care center the next day, she temporarily moved into a room, just down the hall from Sydney and she and Deedee conspired with Nurse to have that old blue and white floral wallpaper taken down out of Sydney's room, replacing both it and the putrid green paint, a belated surprise for her birthday. Sydney rarely showed any outward emotion anymore but she was overcome to the point of tears that evening. They had chosen the mint-green she'd always wanted for her kitchen. The painters finished it all in a day. The spot on the wall where the cross had been was replaced by the three miniature bouquets of framed dried flowers, under glass, that Mum had left her when she'd died.

    Sydney had to move some of her personal belongings for the painters. Helka helped her and when she saw the record of Chopin and the ratty old photograph of Elliott on Sydney's night table she stopped and held them in her hands for a long time and she started to cry. She set them back down on the table and sat on the bed next to Sydney. She pulled Sydney toward her and wrapped her arms around her. She asked Sydney how long she was going to carry this weight around with her. This weight of heavy tragedy she should have shed long ago. She told her she was going to have to 'suck it up, buttercup' as old Mrs. Abercrombie used to say in homeroom. She said it has to be forgiveness. That it was the only thing to set her free because Sydney no longer had faith in God, it had to be forgiveness.

    Helka went to Sydney's closet and pulled out the old black mesh bag that Spencer had used when he went fishing. She threw the Chopin record into the bag, followed by the photograph of Elliott. Sydney started to protest but Helka yanked the bag away and Sydney went limp.

"You've got to shake it before you meet the maker," Helka said.

She opened the bureau drawer. She spotted the grey wool sock.

"This too? You've kept this all these years? She threw it into the bag. She opened the top flap a little wider and picked up the record player and pushed it into the bag as well.

"That too?" Sydney whimpered, in a tone of surrender.

"Aye, the stereo too. You can buy yourself a new one to go with your new piece of music; too much association there with this one. Now, come on, get dressed. We need to go out for a ceremony."

"Where to?" asked Sydney.

She was too tired to fight back. Having all these things so close to her all the time and Helka there too.

"Down to the river, down to the river."

Sydney slipped out of her floral granny gown and into a pair of navy blue stretch pants, a white undershirt, and her old grey sweater she used to wear when she raked the fall leaves. She slipped on her ankle-high gardening boots.

"OK. I'm ready."

Helka and Sydney trudged down to the river, in silence, both looking straight ahead.

Sydney didn't want to admit it but she was beginning to feel a sense of relief.

Helka carried the black sports bag on the other side of her, away from Sydney, in case she tried to change her mind but Sydney knew she wouldn't. She wanted this. She had wanted this for a long time and now it seemed someone cared enough about her to want to help her or maybe it was just that she'd been too blind to see it until now.

When they arrived at the edge of Current River, Helka waded right in, shoes and all. Sydney hesitated.

"C'mon!" ordered Helka.

Sydney waded in beside her and felt the icy water churning over her ankles. Her socks and boots were soaked instantly, holding her firmly in place like shackles.

"All right," Helka said. "I'm going to hand you each item, one by one, and with each one I want you to hold it above your head and before you toss it into the water, I want you to perform an act of forgiveness."

Sydney asked her what she meant by performing an act of forgiveness.

"Well, close your eyes, say some words. Speak to him. Say his name. Say, Elliott Edmond Caldwell, I forgive you. Something like that."

Helka handed Sydney the Chopin record first.

"OK, let's start with this."

Sydney closed her eyes and held the record between her hands above her head. She was silent.

"Well?" said Helka.

"Uh...I can't think when my feet are freezing," Sydney said.

"Think of something good in your life, something that would never have happened if this hadn't happened first—if you hadn't met Elliott Caldwell first."

"Elliott Caldwell..." Sydney hesitated. Breathed out. She closed her eyes.

"If I hadn't met you, I most likely would never have spent my life listening to this beautiful music. Chopin. Chopin's *Nocturne*. Spencer never would have played it."

Sydney threw the record into the water. "Elliott Caldwell, I forgive you," she said. After a few minutes, she opened her eyes and looked at Helka. She felt a little exhausted and a little sad.

"OK, great, that was great Sydney. How do you feel?"

"I feel numb and cold," Sydney said.

"Are you ready for the next one?"

"Yes."

"OK, here then." Helka handed Sydney the grey wool sock.

Sydney lifted it to her nose and breathed in. "Agh. What the heck am I doing anyhow?"

She held the sock up over her head and thought for a moment. She thought about the little sip of cherry brandy, she thought about Elliott Caldwell being the *impresario*, she thought about that last night when they had made love.

"Elliott Edmond Caldwell I am hereby letting you go. I am giving back the only piece of you that I have left. If it weren't for you, I may just as well have had a whole lifetime of nothing special." She choked back tears. "I forgive you," she said softly.

Helka turned away and bit at her lip. Sydney knew Helka could tell how hard this was for her. She wanted to embrace her but she knew she needed to continue, to finish this once and for all. Helka pulled the ratty photograph of Elliott from the bag and held it in her hands. This would be the most difficult one for Sydney. Helka handed it to her slowly.

Sydney took the photograph and stared at it. She closed her eyes. She felt twenty-one again and pictured herself in her chocolate-brown sweater, her white blouse, her wool skirt and stockings, lace-up boots. Her hair was still dark and curled into a perm. The string of pearls was on her neck. The frog charm Spencer had given her hung in the center of the necklace. The thought of it gave her strength. She held the photograph over her head.

She'd have this photograph emblazoned into her memory forever. It was there when she woke up in the morning and there when she fell asleep at night. She thought of the frog charm. She thought of Spencer.

"Aw, what's the use," she said. "He was never mine, anyway."

"You don't know that, Sydney. You don't know if he didn't think of you every single day of his life. You don't know if he didn't suffer too. How hard it might have been to stay away."

Sydney shivered.

"What would you want to say to him now, if you could?" Helka said.

Sydney thought for a moment. If she had never met Elliott, she would never have married Spencer. She would have waited for someone else then, who knows what her life would have been.

River of Forgiveness

"Elliott Caldwell, I forgive you," she whispered at the sky. "I forgive you," she almost shouted as she tore the photograph into little pieces and watched them float away, down the river.

Helka praised her and told her she was proud of her. The hardest part was over now. Helka dug the stereo out of the black bag and handed Sydney a speaker.

Sydney told Helka back then, at the Black Fox Inn, she should have tried to understand, to offer him forgiveness. She threw the speaker into the water. She grabbed the other one out of the bag before Helka had time to hand it to her.

"Would you go back and change it now if you could, Sydney? That's all that matters," Helka said.

"No, never. I would not have changed a thing. I cannot imagine never knowing my quiet love with Spencer."

She threw the speaker toward where the other one was now floating downstream. It landed on a rock and teetered there, just for a moment, then tipped into the river and was washed away. She felt a sense of calm, a release. She picked up the stereo and wrapped the cords around it, neatly.

She looked up to the sky and, once again told Elliott Caldwell she forgave him. She could see now how she had made herself the center of attention all these years, exacting sympathy through her self-pity, while she'd been feeling sorry for herself.

She stood with the stereo between her hands, in front of her.

"What is it?" asked Helka.

Sydney didn't speak. All these years she thought he owed her. For her whole life, she felt he owed her for taking away her life. She'd spent her whole life waiting for someone else to make her happy, weighing the burden of her life on someone else; but with Elliott, when he used to make her feel as if she couldn't or didn't like herself, it would not have been possible for her to be happy. It would never have been any good.

She found herself only now, able to realize it is she who must walk her own journey, fill herself up—in the repainting of her walls by Nurse, in last week blowing out her candles and in Helka being here with her now, these were her reasons for living. Sydney dropped the stereo into the water as though releasing a dead weight and headed back for shore, stopping when they were halfway back.

"I can't believe it," she said. "After all this time, I still can't believe the cruel and beautiful nature of love." She stood for a long while, with the water rushing around her feet until she began to shiver. She smelled the fish-tainted scent of the river, heard the current burbling over the stones and branches, travelling along its bed, back to the ocean. She wrapped her arms around herself. She started to say something else then stopped, mid-sentence. She looked down, peering closely at the rotting moss rippling over the stones.

"What?" asked Helka. "What is it?"

Sydney hesitated. "Ah, nothing. It's nothing. Let's go."

Helka tossed the black bag into the garbage can at the edge of the river, next to the picnic tables and she and Sydney slopped, arm in arm, down the path, in their soggy socks and shoes. They reached the road, veering back up toward the care center and Sydney stopped abruptly.

"What now?" Helka asked.

"Ssshhh," Sydney commanded.

They listened.

"I don't hear anything," whispered Helka.

Sydney smiled. She put her hand to her ear and cocked her head in the direction of the river.

"I can hear it." Sydney beamed. "I can hear his song. Chopin. It's Chopin's *Nocturne*. I can hear his song coming up from the river."

Helka was silent.

"Whenever I want to be near him, I can just come back, down here, to the river."

Helka shook her head and put her arm around Sydney and they continued walking down the path and around the bend, through the springtime fields, eclipsing their way toward the end of things; a sense of peace filled them both, a sense of place, a knowing, a belonging for a lifetime—an understanding shared between the two old friends they were.

Kiidumae

IF

If freckles were lovely, and day was night,

And measles were nice and a lie warn't a lie,
Life would be delight, —
But things couldn't go right
For in such a sad plight
I wouldn't be **I**.

If earth was heaven, and now was hence,
And past was present, and false was true,
There might be some sense
But I'd be in suspense
For on such a pretense
You wouldn't be **you**.

If fear was plucky, and globes were square,
And dirt was cleanly and tears were glee
Things would seem fair,—
Yet they'd all despair,
For if here was there
We wouldn't be **we**.

e.e. cummings

CREDIT LINE: "i carry your heart with me(i carry it in". Copyright 1952, (c) 1980, 1991 by the Trustees for the E. E. Cummings Trust, "i like my body when it is with your". Copyright 1923, 1925, 1951, 1953, (c) 1991 by the Trustees for the E. E. Cummings Trust. Copyright (c) 1976 by George James Firmage, "IF". Copyright © 1973, 1983, 1991 by the Trustees for the E. E. Cummings Trust. Copyright (c) 1973, 1983 by George James Firmage, "somewhere i have never travelled,gladly beyond". Copyright 1931, (c) 1959, 1991 by the Trustees for the E. E. Cummings Trust. Copyright (c) 1979 by George James Firmage, "your homecoming will be my homecoming—". Copyright © 1961, 1989, 1991 by the Trustees for the E. E. Cummings Trust, from COMPLETE POEMS: 1904-1962 by E. E. Cummings, edited by George J. Firmage. Used by permission of Liveright Publishing Corporation.

About the Author

K. Lorraine Kiidumae is a graduate of the Humber College School of Creative & Performing Arts. Her work has appeared in various anthologies and literary magazines in the UK, USA, and Canada. She works from her home in the small seaside resort of Nanoose Bay off the Ballenas-Winchelsea archipelago on the eastern shore of central Vancouver Island. She is currently pursuing her Master of Arts (MA) in Creative and Critical Writing with the University of Gloucestershire (UK). *River of Forgiveness* is her first book.

www.ingramcontent.com/pod-product-compliance
Lightning Source LLC
Chambersburg PA
CBHW070545010526
44118CB00012B/1234